Favorite Brand Name™

Gifts from the

KITCHEN

Publications International, Ltd.

Favorite Brand Name Recipes at www.fbnr.com

Microwave Cooking: Microwave ovens vary in wattage. Use the cooking times as guidelines and check for doneness before adding more time.

Preparation/Cooking Times: Preparation times are based on the approximate amount of time required to assemble the recipe before cooking, baking, chilling or serving. These times include preparation steps such as measuring, chopping and mixing. The fact that some preparations and cooking can be done simultaneously is taken into account. Preparation of optional ingredients and serving suggestions is not included.

Contents

Gift-Giving Tips

Get Back to Basics

No matter what you're preparing, beautiful food starts with good cooking and baking basics. Here are some guidelines to keep in mind when you're ready to get started.

- Before beginning, read the entire recipe to make sure you have all the necessary ingredients, utensils and supplies.

- For best results, use the ingredients called for in the recipe. For example, butter, margarine and shortening are not always interchangeable.

- Measure all the ingredients accurately and assemble them in the order they are called for in the recipe.

- Follow the recipe directions and cooking or baking times exactly. Check for doneness using the test given in the recipe.

- Always use the pan or dish size specified in each recipe. Using a different size pan or dish may cause under or overcooking, or sticking and burnt edges.

- Before baking, adjust the oven racks and preheat the oven. Check the oven temperature for accuracy with an oven thermometer.

The Perfect Package

Homemade goodies from your kitchen are a thoughtful gift for any occasion. Make your food gifts extraordinary by wrapping them in unique packages and using decorative accessories. Remember to always use food-safe containers with airtight lids and make sure containers are completely dry before filling them with food or ingredients.

Airtight Canisters: These containers are available in a variety of materials, including glass and plastic. They are great for storing snack mixes, cookies and candies.

Baskets & Boxes: These versatile hold-alls are available in a wide variety of materials and sizes. Wrap plain boxes in decorative papers. Large, sturdy baskets and boxes are well-suited for packing entire themed gifts.

Glass Bottles: Airtight bottles are perfect for barbecue or other types of sauces or salad dressings. Always choose securely stoppered bottles to help prevent leakage.

Glass Jars: Jars are wonderful for presenting mustards, chutneys, snack mixes and cookie mixes. Make sure that the jars have airtight lids.

Gift Bags: These handy totes come in a wide variety of sizes and colors. Pack individual cookies and candies in smaller bags; pack goody-filled jars or canisters in larger bags.

Tins: Metal containers with tight-fitting lids are just the right choice for snack mixes, cookies, candies and truffles. They also hold up well when sent through the mail.

Finishing Touches

After the goodies are made and tucked into pretty packages, you're ready to put the finishing touches on your gift.

Cellophane: This is an indispensable material for hard-to-wrap gifts such as plates of food, individual breads and candies. Gather the ends and secure with a multitude of pretty ribbons.

Decorative Papers: Papers come in a variety of finishes, including glossy and metallic, and many can be enhanced with rubber stamps. Colorful tissue papers are perfect for tucking into gift boxes and bags.

Gift Tags: Tags come in handy when making personalized notes and cards for your gifts. They also make great labels for storing directions, serving suggestions or even the recipe.

Raffia: Tuck assorted colors of raffia into boxes, baskets and pails. Or, use it as ribbon and tie boxes and tins with rustic bows.

Ribbons, Satin Cords and Strings: Thick, colorful ribbons, metallic strings and thin shiny cords add a touch of glamour to any kind of wrapping paper.

Rubber Stamps: Stamps with food or holiday themes paired with colorful inks are perfect for decorating plain papers. They are also great for making personalized note cards for recipes, labels for sauces and jams, storing directions, and gift tags.

Special Instructions

Before giving your gifts, remember to include storage directions for perishable items, especially those that must be refrigerated. It is also nice to include serving suggestions with food gifts, or even the recipe itself.

Special Delivery

When sending edible gifts, proper food selection and packaging is important.

- Moist quick breads and sturdy cookies are ideal choices, as are many non-fragile confections such as fudge and caramels.

- Brownies and bar cookies are generally sturdy, but avoid shipping those with moist fillings and frostings since they become sticky at room temperature. For the same reason, shipping anything with chocolate during the summer or to warm climates is also risky.

- When sending cookies, wrap each type of cookie separately to retain flavors and textures. Cookies can also be wrapped back-to-back in pairs with either plastic wrap or foil.

- It is best to prepare foods just before packing and mailing. Foods should be completely cool before wrapping and packing.

- Wrap all breakable containers in bubble wrap.

- Fill the bottom of a sturdy shipping box with an even layer of packing material. Do not use popped popcorn or puffed cereal as it may attract insects. Place the wrapped foods or containers as snugly as possible inside. Then place crumpled waxed paper, newspaper or paper toweling in between the individual wrapped foods or containers. Fill any crevices with packing material, and add a final layer at the top of the box.

- Ship your food gifts to arrive as soon as possible.

Sweet & Savory Snacks

S'More Gorp

2 cups honey graham cereal
2 cups low-fat granola cereal
2 cups crispy multi-bran cereal squares
2 tablespoons reduced-calorie margarine
1 tablespoon honey
¼ teaspoon ground cinnamon
¾ cup miniature marshmallows
½ cup dried fruit bits or raisins
¼ cup mini semisweet chocolate chips

1. Preheat oven to 275°F.

2. Combine cereals in nonstick 15×10×1-inch jelly-roll pan. Melt margarine in small saucepan; stir in honey and cinnamon. Pour margarine mixture evenly over cereal mixture; toss until cereals are well coated. Spread mixture evenly onto bottom of pan.

3. Bake 35 to 40 minutes or until crisp, stirring after 20 minutes. Cool completely.

4. Add marshmallows, fruit bits and chocolate chips; toss to mix.

Makes 16 servings

S'More Gorp

Cashew & Pretzel Toffee Clusters

¾ cup packed brown sugar
¾ cup light corn syrup
½ cup butter
2 teaspoons vanilla
4 cups tiny pretzel twists (not sticks)
4 cups bite-sized toasted wheat squares cereal
1 can (10 ounces) salted cashew halves and pieces

1. Preheat oven to 300°F. Spray large baking sheet with nonstick cooking spray.

2. Place brown sugar, corn syrup and butter in heavy small saucepan. Heat over medium heat until mixture boils and sugar dissolves, stirring frequently. Remove from heat; stir in vanilla.

3. Combine pretzels, cereal and cashews in large bowl. Pour sugar mixture over pretzel mixture; toss to coat evenly. Spread on prepared baking sheet. Bake 30 minutes, stirring after 15 minutes. Spread onto greased waxed paper. Cool completely; break into clusters. Store in airtight container at room temperature.   *Makes about 8 cups clusters*

Marshall's Garlic Popcorn

10 to 12 cloves garlic, thinly sliced
 4 to 5 tablespoons vegetable oil
½ cup NEWMAN'S OWN® Oldstyle Picture Show Popcorn
 1 tablespoon butter
   Garlic salt
   Parmesan cheese (optional)

Rub garlic slices over bottom of an electric (oil) corn popper. Cook and stir garlic slices with oil in small skillet until golden brown. Drain to remove the garlic slices, reserving oil and garlic separately. Pour the oil into the corn popper. Add NEWMAN'S OWN® Oldstyle Picture Show Popcorn and pop as usual. Melt butter; combine with reserved garlic. After the popping is completed, place popcorn in serving bowl. Toss with garlic butter; season with garlic salt and Parmesan cheese, if desired.   *Makes 4 servings*

Cashew & Pretzel
Toffee Clusters

Sesame Italian Breadsticks

¼ cup grated Parmesan cheese
3 tablespoons sesame seeds
2 teaspoons Italian seasoning
1 teaspoon kosher salt (optional)
12 frozen bread dough dinner rolls, thawed
¼ cup butter, melted

1. Preheat oven to 425°F. Spray large baking sheet with nonstick cooking spray.

2. In small bowl, combine cheese, sesame seeds, Italian seasoning and salt, if desired. Spread out on plate.

3. On lightly floured surface, roll each dinner roll into rope, about 8 inches long and ½ inch thick. Place on baking sheet and brush tops and sides with butter. Roll each buttered rope in seasoning, pressing seasoning into sides. Return ropes to baking sheet, placing 2 inches apart. Twist each rope 3 times, pressing both ends of rope down on baking sheet. Bake 10 to 12 minutes, or until golden brown. *Makes 12 breadsticks*

Hot 'n' Spicy Italian Stix Mix
Prep Time: *15 minutes* • ***Cook Time:*** *30 minutes*

6 tablespoons butter or margarine, melted
2 tablespoons *Frank's® RedHot®* Cayenne Pepper Sauce
1 tablespoon *French's®* Worcestershire Sauce
2⅔ cups *French's®* French Fried Onions, divided
2 cans (1½ ounces each) *French's®* Potato Sticks
4 cups oven-toasted rice cereal squares
1 package (1.25 ounces) Italian spaghetti sauce mix
¼ cup grated Parmesan cheese

1. Preheat oven to 250°F. Combine butter, *Frank's RedHot* Sauce and Worcestershire in glass measuring cup. Place remaining ingredients in shallow roasting pan; mix well. Pour butter mixture over cereal mixture; toss to coat evenly.

2. Bake 30 minutes or until crispy, stirring twice. Cool completely.
Makes 7 cups mix

Sesame Italian Breadsticks

Chocolate-Dipped Delights

1⅔ cups (about 10 ounces) chopped white chocolate
2 cups (about 12 ounces) chopped semisweet chocolate
1⅔ cups (about 10 ounces) chopped milk chocolate
3 tablespoons shortening, divided
Heart-shaped pretzels
1 cup chopped toasted almonds
Biscotti
Chocolate sandwich cookies
Ridged potato chips
Small, clean craft paintbrush

1. To melt chocolate, place each kind of chocolate and 1 tablespoon shortening in separate 4-cup glass measuring cups. Microwave, 1 measuring cup at a time, at MEDIUM (50% power) 4 to 5 minutes or until chocolate is melted, stirring after 2 minutes.

2. Place large sheet waxed paper on counter. Dip ½ of each pretzel into white chocolate. Gently shake off excess chocolate; place on waxed paper. Let stand 10 minutes; repeat to double-dip. Let stand 30 minutes or until set.

3. Dip other halves of pretzels into semisweet chocolate. Place on waxed paper. Let stand until set.

4. Place almonds in medium bowl. Spread milk chocolate on curved edge of biscotti with small knife. Roll in almonds. Place on waxed paper. Let stand 30 minutes or until set.

5. Holding sandwich cookie flat, dip 1 side of each cookie into semisweet chocolate. Shake off excess chocolate. Place on waxed paper. Let stand 30 minutes or until set. Repeat with second side.

6. To paint potato chips, dip small, clean craft paintbrush into melted milk chocolate. Paint chocolate onto 1 side of each chip. Let stand 30 minutes or until set.

7. Store loosely covered at room temperature up to 1 week.

Makes 3 cups melted chocolate

Cheese Straws

3 cups all-purpose flour
¾ teaspoon cayenne pepper
½ teaspoon salt
1 Butter Flavor CRISCO® Stick or 1 cup Butter Flavor CRISCO®
    all-vegetable shortening
3 cups grated Parmesan cheese
3 egg yolks
4 tablespoons cold water

1. Combine flour, pepper and salt in mixing bowl. Cut in shortening using a pastry blender (or 2 knives) until mixture resembles coarse crumbs. Add cheese.

2. Beat egg yolks with water. Add to flour mixture. Toss to combine until dough forms ball. Divide dough in half. Wrap each half in plastic wrap. Refrigerate at least 1 hour.

3. Heat oven to 375°F. Place sheets of foil on countertop for cooling cheese straws.

4. Spread 1 tablespoon of flour on large sheet of waxed paper. Place one half of dough on floured paper. Flatten slightly with hands. Turn dough over and cover with another large sheet of waxed paper. Roll dough to ¼-inch thickness. Remove top sheet of waxed paper. Cut into strips ½ inch wide. Twist strips. Transfer to ungreased baking sheet with large pancake turner. Place 1 inch apart on ungreased baking sheet. Repeat with remaining dough.

5. Bake one baking sheet at a time at 375°F for 7 to 9 minutes. *Do not overbake.* Cool 2 minutes on baking sheet. Remove cheese straws to foil to cool completely. *Makes 5 to 6 dozen cheese straws*

gift tip

These savory treats are a wonderful gift on their own, or as part of a cheese and cracker, or wine and cheese gift basket. For a pretty presentation, carefully tie a bundle of Cheese Straws together with colorful ribbon.

Taco Popcorn Olé

9 cups air-popped popcorn
 Butter-flavored cooking spray
1 teaspoon chili powder
½ teaspoon salt
½ teaspoon garlic powder
⅛ teaspoon ground red pepper (optional)

1. Preheat oven to 350°F. Line 15×10-inch jelly-roll pan with foil.

2. Place popcorn in single layer in prepared pan. Coat lightly with cooking spray.

3. Combine chili powder, salt, garlic powder and red pepper, if desired, in small bowl; sprinkle over popcorn. Mix lightly to coat evenly.

4. Bake 5 minutes or until hot, stirring gently after 3 minutes. Spread mixture in single layer on large sheet of foil to cool. *Makes 6 (1½-cup) servings*

Note: Store popcorn mixture in a tightly covered container at room temperature up to 4 days.

Spice 'n Sugar Walnuts

1 cup sugar
1 teaspoon LAWRY'S® Seasoned Salt
1 teaspoon cinnamon
½ teaspoon nutmeg
½ teaspoon cloves
½ cup water
2 cups walnut halves

In medium saucepan, combine sugar, Seasoned Salt, spices and water; mix well until sugar dissolves. Bring to a boil over medium-high heat; reduce heat to low and simmer, uncovered, 5 to 7 minutes to soft ball stage (236°F on candy thermometer). Remove from heat and add walnut halves. Stir until walnuts are well coated. Turn out onto waxed paper, separate and cool. Store in an air-tight container. *Makes 2 cups walnuts*

Note: Use 2 cups pecan halves or toasted whole almonds in place of walnuts, if desired.

Taco Popcorn Olé

Parmesan Garlic Twists

⅓ **Butter Flavor CRISCO® Stick or ⅓ cup Butter Flavor CRISCO®**
  all-vegetable shortening plus additional for greasing
 1 **cup all-purpose flour**
½ **teaspoon baking powder**
½ **teaspoon salt**
½ **teaspoon Italian seasoning***
¾ **cup grated Parmesan cheese, divided**
 3 **egg yolks**
 4 **cloves garlic, minced or crushed, or ½ teaspoon garlic powder**
 2 **teaspoons water**
 1 **egg white**
   Paprika

*Or, substitute ½ teaspoon of dried oregano, basil, rosemary or marjoram or some combination of these herbs.

1. Heat oven to 400°F. Grease baking sheets with shortening. Place sheets of foil on countertop for cooling garlic twists.

2. Combine flour, baking powder, salt and Italian seasoning in large bowl. Reserve 1 tablespoon Parmesan cheese. Add remaining cheese to flour mixture. Cut in ⅓ cup shortening with pastry blender (or two knives) until mixture resembles coarse crumbs. Beat egg yolks, garlic and water lightly. Sprinkle over flour mixture. Toss lightly with fork until dough forms ball. Flour lightly.

3. Roll dough out on floured surface or between two sheets of waxed paper to form 13×9-inch rectangle. Trim edges to straighten.

4. Cut in half crosswise. Cut strips ¼ inch wide (they will be 6½ inches long). Twist two strips together, overlapping each strip over the other. Place 2 inches apart on prepared baking sheets. Repeat until all strips are twists. Brush with egg white. Sprinkle with reserved Parmesan cheese.

5. Bake at 400°F for 8 to 10 minutes or until lightly browned. *Do not overbake.* Cool one minute. Remove to foil to cool completely. Sprinkle with paprika.

Makes 3 dozen twists

Note: Serve these twists with your favorite chunky pasta sauce.

Parmesan Garlic Twists

Pastel Popcorn

2½ quarts popped popcorn
½ cup corn syrup
⅓ cup water
1 cup sugar
½ teaspoon salt
¼ cup butter or margarine, cut into pieces
1 teaspoon vanilla
Food coloring

1. Pour popcorn into large heat-proof bowl; set aside.

2. Combine corn syrup, water, sugar and salt in medium saucepan. Cook over medium heat, stirring constantly, until sugar dissolves and mixture comes to a boil. Wash down side of pan frequently with pastry brush dipped in hot water to remove sugar crystals.

3. Add candy thermometer. Continue to cook until mixture reaches hard-ball stage (255°F). Remove from heat.

4. Whisk in butter and vanilla. Add food coloring, a few drops at a time, until desired color is obtained. Immediately pour sugar mixture over popcorn, stirring until completely coated. Spread popcorn on 2 large baking sheets.

5. Cool slightly and shape in balls or leave as clusters.

Makes about 2½ quarts popcorn

Note: Remove any unpopped kernels before measuring the popped popcorn.

Kool-Pop Treat

1 (3-ounce) bag ORVILLE REDENBACHER'S® Microwave Popping Corn, popped according to package directions
2 cups brightly colored puffed oat cereal, such as fruit flavored loops
2 cups miniature marshmallows
1 (.35-ounce) package strawberry soft drink mix
2 tablespoons powdered sugar

1. In large bowl, combine popcorn, cereal and marshmallows.

2. Combine drink mix and powdered sugar; sift over popcorn mixture. Toss to coat.

Makes 12 (1-cup) servings

Pastel Popcorn

Easy Italian No-Bake Snack Mix

Prep Time: 10 minutes

    3 tablespoons olive oil
    1 tablespoon dried Italian seasoning
    1 box (7 ounces) baked crispy snack crackers
    4 cups small bow tie pretzels
    1 can (12 ounces) cocktail peanuts
    ¼ cup grated Parmesan cheese

1. Combine oil and seasoning in large resealable plastic food storage bag; knead well.

2. Add crackers, pretzels and peanuts. Seal bag; shake gently to coat well with oil mixture. Add cheese. Seal bag; shake gently to combine. Snack mix can be stored in bag up to 5 days.

Makes 10 cups snack mix

Oat and Apple Granola

    4 cups old-fashioned oats
    ½ cup sunflower seeds
    ¼ teaspoon salt
    1 cup apple juice concentrate, thawed
    ¼ cup honey
    1 tablespoon canola oil
    ¼ cup dried apples, diced
    ¼ cup raisins
    ¼ cup dried cranberries, blueberries or cherries

Preheat oven to 350°F. Lightly oil 15×10-inch jelly-roll pan.

In large bowl, combine oats, sunflower seeds and salt. In large measuring cup, blend apple juice concentrate, honey and canola oil. Drizzle liquid mixture over oat mixture and toss until evenly coated. Spread on prepared pan.

Bake 30 to 35 minutes, stirring every 5 minutes, until light golden and crisp. Transfer to large bowl. Add dried fruit and toss to mix. Cool completely. Store in tightly covered container for 1 week, or in freezer for up to 2 months.

Makes 12 (½-cup) servings

Favorite recipe from **Canada's Canola Industry**

Easy Italian No-Bake Snack Mix

Caramel Popcorn Balls

16 cups plain popped popcorn (do not use buttered popcorn)
1 package (14 ounces) caramels, unwrapped
¼ cup butter
  Pinch of salt
1⅔ cups shredded sweetened coconut
1 package (12 ounces) semisweet chocolate chips
10 to 12 lollipop sticks
  Assorted colored sprinkles

1. Place popcorn in large bowl.

2. In medium saucepan over low heat, place caramels and butter. Cook and stir until caramels and butter are melted and smooth, about 5 minutes. Stir in salt and coconut. Remove caramel mixture from heat; pour over popcorn. With large wooden spoon, mix until popcorn is evenly coated. Let cool slightly.

3. Place chocolate chips in microwavable bowl. Microwave at HIGH 1 minute; stir. Microwave at HIGH for additional 30-second intervals until chips are completely melted, stirring after each 30-second interval. Stir until smooth.

4. When popcorn mixture is cool enough to handle, grease hands with butter or nonstick cooking spray. Shape popcorn mixture into baseball-sized balls; place 1 lollipop stick in each ball. Dip each popcorn ball into melted chocolate and roll in assorted sprinkles. Place on waxed paper until chocolate is set.

Makes 10 to 12 balls

Roasted Almonds

2 tablespoons CRISCO® Canola Oil, divided
1 pound whole blanched almonds
2 teaspoons ground cinnamon
  Confectioners' sugar

1. Heat 1 tablespoon oil in large skillet over medium heat until hot. Add ½ pound almonds. Cook and stir until evenly browned. Sprinkle with 1 teaspoon cinnamon; stir well. Place on paper towels to drain. Dust with confectioners' sugar to taste.

2. Repeat with remaining ingredients.

Makes 1 pound nuts

Cocoa Snackin' Jacks

1 (3-ounce) bag ORVILLE REDENBACHER'S® Microwave Popping Corn,
     popped according to package instructions
½ cup crumbled reduced fat chocolate cookies
½ cup granulated sugar
½ cup firmly packed brown sugar
¼ cup light corn syrup
2 tablespoons reduced fat margarine
1 tablespoon water
¼ teaspoon cream of tartar
1 (.53-oz) package SWISS MISS® Fat Free Hot Cocoa Mix
1 teaspoon baking soda

1. In large bowl, combine Orville Redenbacher's Popped Corn and cookies; set aside.

2. In medium saucepan, combine sugars, syrup, margarine, water and cream of tartar.

3. Bring to a boil and stir constantly until candy thermometer reaches 260°F. Remove from heat.

4. Quickly add Swiss Miss Cocoa and baking soda; stir thoroughly.

5. Working quickly, pour mixture over popcorn and cookie mixture. Gently toss to coat.

6. Spread mixture onto waxed paper to cool and harden. Break into pieces.

Makes 16 (1-ounce) servings

Ortega® Snack Mix

3 cups lightly salted peanuts
3 cups corn chips
3 cups spoon-size shredded wheat cereal
2 cups lightly salted pretzels
1 package (1.25 ounces) ORTEGA® Taco Seasoning Mix
¼ cup (½ stick) butter or margarine, melted

COMBINE peanuts, corn chips, shredded wheat, pretzels, seasoning mix and butter in large bowl; toss well to coat. Store in airtight container or zipper-type plastic bag.

Makes about 20 servings

Spiced Sesame Wonton Crisps

20 (3-inch-square) wonton wrappers, cut in half
1 tablespoon water
2 teaspoons olive oil
½ teaspoon paprika
½ teaspoon ground cumin or chili powder
¼ teaspoon dry mustard
1 tablespoon sesame seeds

1. Preheat oven to 375°F. Coat 2 large nonstick baking sheets with nonstick cooking spray.

2. Cut each halved wonton wrapper into 2 strips; place in single layer on prepared baking sheets.

3. Combine water, oil, paprika, cumin and mustard in small bowl; mix well. Brush oil mixture evenly onto wonton strips; sprinkle evenly with sesame seeds.

4. Bake 6 to 8 minutes or until lightly browned. Remove to wire rack; cool completely. Transfer to serving plate. *Makes 8 servings*

Magic Wands

1 cup semisweet chocolate chips
12 pretzel rods
3 ounces white chocolate baking bars or confectionery coating
Food color
Assorted sprinkles

1. Line baking sheet with waxed paper.

2. Melt chocolate chips in top of double boiler over hot, not boiling, water. Remove from heat. Dip pretzel rods into chocolate, spooning chocolate to coat about ¾ of each pretzel. Place on prepared baking sheet. Refrigerate until chocolate is firm.

3. Melt white chocolate in top of clean double boiler over hot, not boiling, water. Stir in food color to make desired color. Remove from heat. Dip coated pretzels quickly into colored white chocolate to coat about ¼ of each pretzel.

4. Place on baking sheet. Immediately top with sprinkles. Refrigerate until chocolate is firm. *Makes 12 wands*

Spiced Sesame Wonton Crisps

Honey Popcorn Clusters

Vegetable cooking spray
6 cups air-popped popcorn
⅔ cup DOLE® Golden or Seedless Raisins
½ cup DOLE® Chopped Dates or Pitted Dates, chopped
⅓ cup almonds (optional)
⅓ cup packed brown sugar
¼ cup honey
2 tablespoons margarine
¼ teaspoon baking soda

• Line bottom and sides of 13×9-inch baking pan with large sheet of aluminum foil. Spray foil with vegetable cooking spray.

• Stir together popcorn, raisins, dates and almonds in foil-lined pan.

• Combine brown sugar, honey and margarine in small saucepan. Bring to boil over medium heat, stirring constantly; reduce heat to low. Cook 5 minutes. *Do not stir.* Remove from heat.

• Stir in baking soda. Pour evenly over popcorn mixture, stirring quickly to coat mixture evenly.

• Bake at 300°F 12 to 15 minutes or until mixture is lightly browned, stirring once halfway through baking time.

• Lift foil from pan; place on cooling rack. Cool popcorn mixture completely; break into clusters. Popcorn can be stored in airtight container up to 1 week.

Makes 7 cups clusters

Roasted Nuts from Hidden Valley®

1 pound assorted unsalted nuts, such as pecans, walnuts or mixed nuts
¼ cup maple syrup
2 tablespoons light brown sugar
1 packet (1 ounce) HIDDEN VALLEY® The Original Ranch® Salad Dressing & Seasoning Mix

Place nuts in plastic bag; add maple syrup and coat well. Sprinkle sugar and salad dressing & seasoning mix over nuts. Coat well. Spread nuts in single layer on greased baking pan. Bake at 250°F for 35 minutes. Transfer immediately to large bowl. Cool, stirring to separate.

Makes about 4 cups nuts

Honey Popcorn Clusters

Turtle Caramel Apples

4 large Golden Delicious or Granny Smith apples
4 craft sticks (available where cake decorating supplies are sold)
1 package (14 ounces) caramels, unwrapped
2 tablespoons water
2 jars (3½ ounces each) macadamia nuts or pecans, coarsely chopped
1 bittersweet or semisweet chocolate candy bar (about 2 ounces), broken
   into small pieces

1. Line 13×9-inch baking pan with waxed paper; set aside.

2. To prepare apples, wash and dry completely. Remove stems. Insert craft sticks into centers of apples.

3. Combine caramels and water in small saucepan. Simmer over low heat until caramels melt and mixture is smooth, stirring frequently.

4. Immediately dip apples, one at a time, into caramel to cover completely. Scrape excess caramel from bottom of apple onto side of saucepan, letting excess drip back into saucepan.

5. Immediately roll apples in nuts to lightly coat, pressing nuts lightly with fingers so they stick to caramel. Place apples, stick-side up, on prepared baking sheet. Let stand 20 minutes or until caramel is set.

6. Place chocolate in small resealable plastic food storage bag; seal bag. Microwave at MEDIUM (50% power) 1 minute. Turn bag over; microwave at MEDIUM 1 minute or until melted. Knead bag until chocolate is smooth. Cut off very tiny corner of bag; pipe or drizzle chocolate decoratively onto apples.

7. Let apples stand 30 minutes or until chocolate is set. Store loosely covered in refrigerator up to 3 days. Let stand at room temperature 15 minutes before serving.

Makes 4 apples

gift tip

To use Turtle Caramel Apples as place cards, first wrap them in clear or colored plastic wrap. Then, simply write each guest's name on a card and attach it to the wrapped apple with ribbon or raffia. Place one apple on each guest's plate.

Turtle Caramel Apples

Sweet Nothings Trail Mix

    5 cups rice and corn cereal squares
1½ cups raisins
1½ cups small thin pretzel sticks, broken into pieces
    1 cup candy-coated chocolate candy
    1 cup peanuts

Combine cereal, raisins, pretzels, candy and peanuts in large resealable plastic food storage bag; shake well. Distribute evenly among resealable plastic food storage bags or serve in large bowl. *Makes 10 cups trail mix*

Note: To use this recipe as a party favor, simply wrap handfuls of trail mix in pink plastic wrap and tie with red, white or pink ribbons.

Walnut-Granola Clusters

¼ cup butter
    1 (10½-ounce) package miniature marshmallows
½ teaspoon ground cinnamon
    3 cups rolled oats
    2 cups chopped California walnuts
    1 cup flaked coconut
    2 (1-ounce) squares semi-sweet chocolate

Microwave butter in large microwavable mixing bowl at HIGH (100% power) 40 seconds or until melted. Stir in marshmallows and cinnamon. Microwave 1½ minutes or until melted, stirring halfway through cooking time. Quickly stir in oats, walnuts and coconut. With wet hands, form mixture into small balls and place on wax paper-lined baking sheets.

Microwave chocolate in glass measuring cup at HIGH 2½ minutes or until melted; stir. Lightly drizzle chocolate over clusters. May be stored at room temperature, uncovered, 4 to 5 days. *Makes 5 dozen clusters*

Favorite recipe from **Walnut Marketing Board**

Sweet Nothings Trail Mix

Breadstick Sampler

1 can (11 ounces) refrigerated breadstick dough (8 breadsticks)
1 tablespoon grated Parmesan cheese
⅛ teaspoon ground red pepper
½ teaspoon dried basil leaves
½ teaspoon dried oregano leaves
½ teaspoon dried thyme leaves
2 tablespoons olive oil
1 tablespoon garlic powder, divided

1. Preheat oven to 350°F. Separate and unroll strips of dough. Twist each breadstick several times and place on greased cookie sheet about 1 inch apart. Press ends firmly onto pans to anchor.

2. Combine cheese and pepper in small bowl. Combine basil, oregano and thyme in another small bowl.

3. Brush all 8 breadsticks with olive oil. Sprinkle 2 breadsticks with 1 teaspoon garlic powder each. Sprinkle 2 breadsticks with 1 teaspoon cheese mixture each. Sprinkle 2 breadsticks with ½ teaspoon herb mixture each. For the last pair of breadsticks, sprinkle each with remaining garlic powder, cheese mixture and herb mixture.

4. Bake 15 minutes or until golden brown. Transfer to wire rack to cool 5 minutes. Serve warm.

Makes 8 breadsticks

Note: You can easily adapt this recipe by sprinkling on your own favorite toppings. Try sesame or poppy seeds, seasoned salt, onion powder or cinnamon and sugar.

Spicy Toasted Nuts

2 tablespoons vegetable oil
1 tablespoon HEINZ® Worcestershire Sauce
1 cup pecan or walnut halves

In bowl, combine oil and Worcestershire sauce; add nuts and toss to coat. Spread nuts in shallow baking pan; drizzle with any remaining oil mixture. Bake in 325°F oven, 15 minutes, stirring occasionally. Sprinkle with salt or garlic salt, if desired.

Makes 1 cup nuts

Breadstick Sampler

Snackin' in Seattle Popcorn

1 (3½-ounce) bag NEWMAN'S OWN® Natural Flavor Microwave Popcorn
1 cup dried tart cherries
1 cup toasted hazelnuts, chopped
¾ cup granulated sugar
10 tablespoons (1¼ sticks) margarine or butter
½ cup packed brown sugar
½ cup dark corn syrup
1 teaspoon ground cinnamon
1 teaspoon instant espresso-coffee powder

Pop popcorn according to package directions. Pour popcorn into greased large roasting pan and stir in dried cherries and hazelnuts.

In 2-quart saucepan, mix granulated sugar, margarine, brown sugar and corn syrup; heat on medium heat, stirring constantly, until temperature reaches 290°F on candy thermometer, about 15 to 20 minutes. Remove from heat and stir in cinnamon and espresso powder. Pour over popcorn mixture and stir well to coat evenly.

Let mixture cool slightly. If desired, while still warm, form into balls. After cooling, store in airtight container.

Makes about 10 cups or 24 popcorn balls

Cranberry Gorp

¼ cup unsalted butter
¼ cup packed light brown sugar
1 tablespoon maple syrup
1 teaspoon curry powder
½ teaspoon ground cinnamon
1½ cups dried cranberries
1½ cups coarsely chopped walnuts and/or slivered almonds
1½ cups lightly salted pretzel nuggets

1. Preheat oven to 300°F. Grease 15×10-inch jelly-roll pan. Combine butter, brown sugar and maple syrup in large saucepan; heat over medium heat until butter is melted. Stir in curry powder and cinnamon. Add cranberries, walnuts and pretzels; stir to combine.

2. Spread mixture on prepared pan. Bake 15 minutes or until mixture is crunchy and light brown.

Makes 20 servings

Caramelized Nuts

1 cup slivered almonds, pecans or walnuts
⅓ cup sugar
½ teaspoon ground cinnamon (optional)
¼ teaspoon grated nutmeg (optional)

1. To toast nuts, cook and stir in medium skillet over medium heat 9 to 12 minutes until light golden brown. Transfer to small bowl.

2. Sprinkle sugar evenly over bottom of skillet. Cook, without stirring, 2 to 4 minutes until sugar is melted. Remove from heat.

3. Quickly add nuts to skillet; sprinkle with cinnamon and nutmeg, if desired. Return to heat; stir until nuts are coated with melted sugar mixture. Transfer to plate; cool completely.

4. Place nuts on cutting board; coarsely chop. Store in airtight container up to 2 weeks. *Makes 1 cup nuts*

Note: Care should be taken when caramelizing sugar because melted sugar can cause serious burns if spilled or splattered.

Krispie Cheese Twists

½ cup grated Parmesan cheese
¾ teaspoon LAWRY'S® Seasoned Pepper
½ teaspoon LAWRY'S® Garlic Powder with Parsley
1 package (17¼ ounces) frozen puff pastry, thawed
1 egg white, lightly beaten

In small bowl, combine Parmesan cheese, Seasoned Pepper and Garlic Powder with Parsley. Unfold pastry sheets onto cutting board. Brush pastry lightly with egg white; sprinkle each sheet with ¼ cheese mixture. Lightly press into pastry, turn over; repeat. Cut into 1-inch strips; twist. Place on greased cookie sheet and bake in 350°F oven 15 minutes or until golden brown.

Makes 2 dozen twists

Note: To make 1 dozen, use one of the two packaged pastry sheets and reduce other ingredients by half.

Cinnamon Caramel Corn

8 cups air-popped popcorn (about ⅓ cup kernels)
2 tablespoons honey
4 teaspoons margarine
¼ teaspoon ground cinnamon

1. Preheat oven to 350°F. Spray jelly-roll pan with nonstick cooking spray. Place popcorn in large bowl.

2. Stir honey, margarine and cinnamon in small saucepan over low heat until margarine is melted and mixture is smooth; immediately pour over popcorn. Toss with spoon to coat evenly. Pour onto prepared pan; bake 12 to 14 minutes or until coating is golden brown and appears crackled, stirring twice. Let cool on pan 5 minutes. (As popcorn cools, coating becomes crisp. If not crisp enough, or if popcorn softens upon standing, return to oven and heat 5 to 8 minutes.) *Makes 4 servings*

Cajun Popcorn: Preheat oven and prepare jelly-roll pan as directed above. Combine 7 teaspoons honey, 4 teaspoons margarine and 1 teaspoon Cajun or Creole seasoning in small saucepan. Proceed with recipe as directed above. Makes 4 servings.

Italian Popcorn: Spray 8 cups of air-popped popcorn with fat-free butter-flavored spray to coat. Sprinkle with 2 tablespoons finely grated Parmesan cheese, ⅛ teaspoon black pepper and ½ teaspoon dried oregano leaves. Gently toss to coat. Makes 4 servings.

Original Ranch® Snack Mix

8 cups KELLOGG'S® CRISPIX®* cereal
2½ cups small pretzels
2½ cups bite-size Cheddar cheese crackers (optional)
3 tablespoons vegetable oil
1 packet (1 ounce) HIDDEN VALLEY® The Original Ranch® Salad Dressing & Seasoning Mix

*Kellogg's® and Crispix® are registered trademarks of Kellogg Company.

Combine cereal, pretzels and crackers in a gallon-size Glad® Zipper Storage Bag. Pour oil over mixture. Seal bag and toss to coat. Add salad dressing & seasoning mix; seal bag and toss again until coated.

Makes 10 cups snack mix

*Clockwise from top: Italian Popcorn,
Cinnamon Caramel Corn and
Cajun Popcorn*

Teddy Bear Party Mix

Prep Time: 5 minutes • Cook Time: 12 minutes

4 cups crisp cinnamon graham cereal
2 cups honey flavored teddy-shaped graham snacks
1 can (1½ ounces) *French's*® Potato Sticks
3 tablespoons melted unsalted butter
2 tablespoons *French's*® Worcestershire Sauce
1 tablespoon packed brown sugar
¼ teaspoon ground cinnamon
1 cup sweetened dried cranberries or raisins
½ cup chocolate, peanut butter or carob chips

1. Preheat oven to 350°F. Lightly spray jelly-roll pan with nonstick cooking spray. Combine cereal, graham snacks and potato sticks in large bowl.

2. Combine butter, Worcestershire, sugar and cinnamon in small bowl; toss with cereal mixture. Transfer to prepared pan. Bake 12 minutes. Cool completely.

3. Stir in dried cranberries and chips. Store in an air-tight container.

Makes about 7 cups snack mix

Honey-Roasted Bridge Mix

Prep Time: about 15 minutes • Bake Time: about 15 minutes

½ cup honey
2 tablespoons butter or margarine
1 teaspoon ground cinnamon, divided
4 cups mixed nuts
2 to 3 tablespoons superfine sugar

Preheat oven to 325°F. Combine honey, butter and ½ teaspoon cinnamon in saucepan. Bring mixture to a boil; cook 2 minutes, stirring constantly. Pour honey mixture over nuts; stir well until nuts are coated. Spread nut mixture onto foil-lined cookie sheet or jelly-roll pan.

Bake 10 to 15 minutes or until nuts are glazed and lightly browned. Do not allow nuts to burn. Cool 20 to 30 minutes; remove from foil. Combine sugar and remaining ½ teaspoon cinnamon; toss with glazed nuts to coat.

Makes 4 cups bridge mix

Favorite recipe from **National Honey Board**

Teddy Bear
Party Mix

Gifts in a Jar

Apricot-Cranberry Bread Mix

2½ cups all-purpose flour
1 cup chopped dried apricots
¾ cup sugar
½ cup dried cranberries
4 teaspoons baking powder
½ teaspoon baking soda
½ teaspoon salt

1. Layer ingredients attractively in any order in 1-quart food storage jar with tight-fitting lid. Pack ingredients down slightly before adding another layer.

2. Cover top of jar with fabric; attach gift tag with recipe below.

Makes one 1-quart jar

Apricot-Cranberry Bread

1 jar Apricot-Cranberry Bread Mix
1¼ cups buttermilk
¼ cup shortening
1 egg, beaten

1. Preheat oven to 350°F. Spray 9×5-inch loaf pan with nonstick cooking spray.

2. Pour contents of jar into large bowl. Combine buttermilk, shortening and egg in small bowl until blended; stir into jar mixture just until moistened. Pour evenly into prepared pan.

3. Bake 45 to 50 minutes or until toothpick inserted in center comes out clean. Cool in pan on wire rack 10 minutes; remove from pan and cool completely on wire rack.

Makes 1 loaf

Apricot-Cranberry Bread

Roasted Vegetable Tomato Sauce

1 eggplant, cut into ¾-inch slices
1½ teaspoons salt, divided
2 zucchini, halved and cut crosswise into ½-inch pieces
2 red or yellow bell peppers, cut into ¾-inch strips
8 ounces small mushrooms, stems trimmed
1 red onion, cut into ¾-inch pieces
¼ cup olive oil
2 tablespoons balsamic vinegar
3 to 4 cloves garlic, minced
1 teaspoon dried rosemary
1 can (28 ounces) tomato sauce
¾ cup water
2 teaspoons sugar
2 teaspoons dried basil leaves
½ teaspoon red pepper flakes

1. Place eggplant slices in large colander set over bowl; sprinkle with 1 teaspoon salt. Drain 30 minutes. Rinse eggplant under cold running water. Pat dry with paper towels. Cut slices crosswise into ¾-inch pieces. Set aside.

2. Preheat oven to 425°F. Combine eggplant, zucchini, bell peppers, mushrooms and onion in 15×10-inch jelly-roll pan.

3. Whisk oil, vinegar, garlic and rosemary in small bowl until well blended; pour over vegetables, stirring until evenly coated.

4. Bake 25 minutes or until vegetables are brown and tender, stirring occasionally. Sprinkle remaining ½ teaspoon salt evenly over vegetables.

5. Meanwhile, combine tomato sauce, water, sugar, basil and pepper flakes in large saucepan. Bring to a boil over high heat. Reduce heat to medium-low; cover. Simmer 10 minutes, stirring occasionally.

6. Add roasted vegetables and cooking liquid to saucepan. Cover; simmer 5 minutes, stirring occasionally. Remove saucepan from heat; cool completely.

7. Store in airtight container in refrigerator up to 5 days.

Makes about 8 cups sauce

Roasted Vegetable Tomato Sauce

Citrus Butter

1 cup butter, softened
¾ teaspoon grated fresh orange peel
2 tablespoons fresh orange juice
¼ teaspoon grated fresh lime peel

1. Combine butter, orange peel, orange juice and lime peel in medium bowl with electric mixer. Beat at medium speed until well blended.

2. Place butter mixture on sheet of waxed paper. Using waxed paper to hold butter mixture, roll it back and forth to form log. Wrap log in plastic wrap.

3. Store in airtight container in refrigerator up to 2 weeks.

Makes about 1 cup butter

Note: To serve, remove desired amount of butter from roll; immediately refrigerate remaining butter.

Honey Butter: Omit orange peel, orange juice and lime peel. Substitute ¼ cup honey.

Strawberry Butter: Omit orange peel, orange juice and lime peel. Substitute ⅔ cup strawberry preserves.

Southwest Vinaigrette

Prep Time: *5 minutes* • **Total Time:** *5 minutes*

¼ cup red wine vinegar
2 tablespoons chopped cilantro or parsley
1 tablespoon chili powder, or to taste
2 teaspoons granulated sugar
½ teaspoon salt
¼ teaspoon freshly ground black pepper
¾ cup CRISCO® Oil*

*Use your favorite Crisco Oil product.

1. Combine vinegar, cilantro, chili powder, sugar, salt and pepper in jar with tight-fitting lid. Shake well. Add oil. Shake again.   *Makes 1 cup vinaigrette*

Note: This dressing can be made up to two days in advance and refrigerated, tightly covered. Shake well just before serving.

Citrus Butter

Buckwheat Pancakes

1 cup Buckwheat Pancake Mix (recipe follows)
1 cup milk
2 tablespoons butter, melted
1 egg, lightly beaten

1. Place pancake mix in medium bowl; make well in center.

2. Whisk together milk, butter and egg in small bowl. Pour into well. Stir mixture just until blended. (Batter will have small lumps.)

3. Lightly grease griddle or skillet with additional butter or nonstick cooking spray. Heat griddle until hot.

4. Drop batter by ¼ cupfuls onto hot griddle. Cook 3 to 4 minutes or until bubbles appear and break on the surface of pancakes. Turn pancakes. Cook 3 to 4 minutes or until bottoms are browned. Serve immediately.

Makes about 12 pancakes

Buckwheat Pancake Mix

2 cups buckwheat flour*
2 cups all-purpose flour
2 tablespoons sugar
4 teaspoons baking powder
2 teaspoons baking soda
1 teaspoon salt

Buckwheat flour can be purchased in health food stores. Substitute whole wheat flour, if desired.

Combine all ingredients in medium bowl until well blended. Store in airtight container at room temperature up to 2 months.   *Makes about 4 cups mix*

Buckwheat Pancakes

Apple & Dried-Cherry Chutney

    3 tablespoons vegetable oil
1½ cups chopped red onions
    1 tablespoon minced fresh ginger
    ¼ teaspoon red pepper flakes
    ⅓ cup dried cherries
    1 tablespoon packed dark brown sugar
    ¼ teaspoon salt
    1 cup water
    1 Washington Granny Smith apple, cored and finely chopped
    1 teaspoon cornstarch dissolved in 1 tablespoon water
    1 teaspoon balsamic vinegar

In large skillet, heat oil over medium heat. Add onions, ginger and pepper flakes; cook and stir 5 minutes. Add dried cherries, brown sugar and salt. Stir in water; cover and cook over medium heat 5 minutes.

Add apple to onion mixture. Cover; cook 6 to 8 minutes or until apple is tender. Stir cornstarch mixture into apple-onion mixture and cook over high heat, stirring constantly, until mixture is thickened and appears glazed, about 1 minute. Remove from heat; stir in vinegar. Cool before serving or storing. Chutney can be refrigerated for one week or frozen for one month.

Makes 2 cups chutney

Favorite recipe from **Washington Apple Commission**

gift tip

Chutney makes a flavorful addition to a gift basket of breads. Serve it plain as a spread, or for a delicious appetizer, spoon it over softened cream cheese and serve with assorted crackers.

Classic Vinaigrette

¼ cup FILIPPO BERIO® Olive Oil
¼ cup white wine vinegar
1 teaspoon Dijon mustard
¼ teaspoon sugar
Salt and freshly ground black pepper

In small screw-topped jar, combine olive oil, vinegar, mustard and sugar. Shake vigorously until well blended. Season to taste with salt and pepper. Store dressing in refrigerator up to 1 week. Shake well before using.

Makes about ½ cup vinaigrette

Garlic Vinaigrette: Add 1 small, halved garlic clove to oil mixture; let stand 1 hour. Discard garlic. Store and serve as directed above.

Lemon Vinaigrette: Use 2 tablespoons lemon juice in place of vinegar; add finely grated peel of 1 small lemon to oil mixture. Store and serve as directed above.

Herb Vinaigrette: Whisk 1 to 2 tablespoons finely chopped fresh herbs (basil, oregano or chives) into dressing just before serving. Store and serve as directed above.

Shallot Vinaigrette: Add 1 to 2 finely chopped shallots to oil mixture; let stand at least 1 hour before serving. Store and serve as directed above.

Honey Caramel Sauce

1 cup honey
1 cup evaporated skim milk
½ cup butter or margarine

Combine honey, milk and butter in medium saucepan; mix well. Cook and stir until mixture comes to a boil. Cook over medium heat 8 to 10 minutes longer or until mixture thickens and becomes caramel colored. Pour into sterilized gift jars. Keep refrigerated.

Makes 2 cups sauce

Favorite recipe from **National Honey Board**

Quick & Easy Couscous Mix

  1 **cup uncooked couscous**
  ¼ **cup dried cranberries**
  ¼ **cup currants**
  2 **tablespoons dried vegetable flakes**
  1 **tablespoon dried minced onion**
  1 **tablespoon dried parsley flakes**
  1 **teaspoon chicken bouillon granules**
  ¾ **teaspoon curry powder**
  ½ **teaspoon salt**
  ½ **teaspoon black pepper**
  ¼ **teaspoon turmeric**
  ¼ **cup slivered almonds**

1. Layer ½ cup couscous, cranberries, currants, vegetable flakes, onion, parsley, bouillon granules, curry powder, salt, pepper, turmeric and remaining ½ cup couscous in 1-pint food storage jar with tight-fitting lid. Place almonds in small food storage bag. Close with twist tie and cut off top of bag. Place bag on top of couscous. Close jar.

2. Cover top of jar with fabric; attach gift tag with recipe below.

Makes one 1-pint jar

Quick & Easy Couscous

  1 **jar Quick & Easy Couscous Mix**
1½ **cups water**
  1 **tablespoon butter**

1. Preheat oven to 350°F.

2. Remove almond packet from jar; set aside.

3. Place water, butter and remaining contents of jar in large saucepan. Bring to a boil. Remove pan from heat; cover and let stand 5 minutes.

4. Meanwhile, toast almonds. Spread nuts on shallow baking pan. Bake 5 to 8 minutes or until nuts are golden brown.

5. Fluff couscous with fork; stir in almonds.

Makes 4 to 5 servings

Quick & Easy Couscous

"M&M's"® Gift Jar Cookie Mix

¾ cup all-purpose flour
1 teaspoon baking soda
½ teaspoon salt
½ teaspoon ground cinnamon
½ cup chopped walnuts
1 cup "M&M's"® Chocolate Mini Baking Bits, divided
½ cup raisins
¾ cup firmly packed light brown sugar
1¼ cups uncooked quick oats

In medium bowl combine flour, baking soda, salt and cinnamon. In 1-quart clear glass jar with tight-fitting resealable lid, layer flour mixture, walnuts, ½ cup "M&M's"® Chocolate Mini Baking Bits, raisins, brown sugar, remaining ½ cup "M&M's"® Chocolate Mini Baking Bits and oats. Seal jar; wrap decoratively. Give as a gift with the following instructions: Preheat oven to 350°F. Lightly grease cookie sheets; set aside. In large bowl beat ¾ cup (1½ sticks) butter, 1 egg and ¾ teaspoon vanilla extract until well blended. Stir in contents of jar until well blended. Roll into 1-inch balls and place about 2 inches apart on prepared cookie sheets. Bake 12 to 15 minutes. Cool 2 minutes on cookie sheets; cool completely on wire racks. Store in tightly covered container. *Makes 4 dozen cookies*

Chunky Applesauce

10 tart apples (about 3 pounds) peeled, cored and chopped
¾ cup packed light brown sugar
½ cup apple juice or apple cider
1½ teaspoons ground cinnamon
⅛ teaspoon salt
⅛ teaspoon ground nutmeg

1. Combine apples, brown sugar, apple juice, cinnamon, salt and nutmeg in heavy, large saucepan; cover. Cook over medium-low heat 40 to 45 minutes or until apples are tender, stirring occasionally. Remove saucepan from heat. Cool completely.

2. Store in airtight container in refrigerator up to 1 month.
Makes about 5½ cups applesauce

"M&M's"® Gift Jar
Cookie Mix

Hearty Chili

1¼ cups dried pinto beans
  1 pound ground beef or turkey
  1 onion, chopped
  3 tablespoons Hearty Chili Seasoning Mix (recipe follows)
  1 can (28 ounces) diced tomatoes, undrained
  1 can (about 14 ounces) beef broth

1. Place beans and 8 cups cold water in large saucepan. Bring to a boil over high heat. Boil 1 minute. Remove saucepan from heat. Cover; let stand 1 hour.

2. Drain beans; rinse under cold running water. Return beans to saucepan. Add 8 cups cold water. Bring to a boil over high heat. Reduce heat to medium-low. Simmer 1 hour 15 minutes or until beans are just tender, stirring occasionally. Remove saucepan from heat and drain beans; set aside.

3. Combine ground beef and onion in large saucepan. Cook over medium-high heat 6 minutes or until beef is no longer pink, stirring to crumble beef. Spoon off and discard any drippings.

4. Add seasoning mix to saucepan. Cook 1 minute, stirring frequently. Add beans, tomatoes with juice and beef broth; bring to a boil over high heat. Reduce heat to medium-low. Cover; simmer 30 minutes, stirring occasionally. Store in airtight container in refrigerator up to 3 days or freeze up to 1 month.

Makes about 8 cups chili

Hearty Chili Seasoning Mix

½ cup chili powder
¼ cup ground cumin
  2 tablespoons garlic salt
  2 tablespoons dried oregano leaves
  2 teaspoons ground coriander
½ teaspoon ground red pepper

Combine all ingredients in small bowl. Store in airtight container at room temperature up to 3 months. *Makes about 1 cup seasoning mix*

Recipe: HEARTY CHILI
       SEASONING MIX

1 CUP CHILI POWDER
½ CUP GROUND CUMIN
2 TABLESPOONS DRIED
2 TABLESPOONS GARLI
2 TEASPOONS GROUND
½ TEASPOON GROUND RE
   PEPPER.

Hearty Chili

Pumpkin Chocolate Chip Muffin Mix

2½ cups all-purpose flour
1 cup packed light brown sugar
1 cup chocolate chips
½ cup chopped walnuts
1 tablespoon baking powder
1½ teaspoons pumpkin pie spice
¼ teaspoon salt

1. Layer ingredients attractively in any order in 1-quart food storage jar with tight-fitting lid. Pack ingredients down slightly before adding another layer.

2. Cover top of jar with fabric; attach gift tag with recipe below.

Makes one 1-quart jar

Pumpkin Chocolate Chip Muffins

1 jar Pumpkin Chocolate Chip Muffin Mix
1 cup canned pumpkin (not pumpkin pie filling)
¾ cup milk
6 tablespoons butter, melted
2 eggs

1. Preheat oven to 400°F. Grease or paper-line 18 regular-size (2½-inch) muffin cups.

2. Pour contents of jar into large bowl. Combine pumpkin, milk, butter and eggs in small bowl until blended; stir into jar mixture just until moistened. Spoon evenly into prepared muffin cups, filling ⅔ full.

3. Bake 15 to 17 minutes or until toothpick inserted in centers comes out clean. Cool in pans on wire racks 10 minutes; remove from pans and cool completely on wire racks.

Makes 18 muffins

Pumpkin Chocolate
Chip Muffins

Cranberry-Apple Chutney

1¼ cups granulated sugar
½ cup water
1 package (12 ounces) fresh or frozen cranberries (about 3½ cups)
2 medium Granny Smith apples, cut into ¼-inch pieces (2 cups)
1 medium onion, chopped
½ cup golden raisins
½ cup packed light brown sugar
¼ cup cider vinegar
1 teaspoon ground ginger
1 teaspoon ground cinnamon
⅛ teaspoon ground allspice
⅛ teaspoon ground cloves
½ cup walnuts or pecans, toasted and chopped

1. Combine granulated sugar and water in heavy 2-quart saucepan. Bring to a boil over high heat. Boil gently 3 minutes. Add cranberries, apples, onion, raisins, brown sugar, vinegar, ginger, cinnamon, allspice and cloves.

2. Bring to a boil over high heat. Reduce heat to medium. Simmer, uncovered, 20 to 25 minutes or until mixture is very thick, stirring occasionally. Cool; stir in walnuts. Cover and refrigerate up to 2 weeks before serving.

Makes about 4 cups chutney

Note: This chutney makes a wonderful appetizer when spooned over cream cheese spread on melba rounds.

Oriental Ginger Dressing

½ cup pineapple juice
2 tablespoons cider vinegar
1 tablespoon sugar
1 tablespoon soy sauce
1 teaspoon grated fresh ginger
½ teaspoon sesame oil

Combine all ingredients in a jar. Cover and shake vigorously. (Or combine ingredients in food processor.) Chill or serve over green salad, chicken salad or pasta salad.

Makes 4 servings

Favorite recipe from **The Sugar Association, Inc.**

Cranberry-Apple
Chutney

Country Six Bean Soup Mix

½ **cup dried baby lima beans**
½ **cup dried kidney beans**
½ **cup dried Great Northern beans**
½ **cup dried red beans**
½ **cup dried navy beans**
½ **cup dried pinto beans**
2 **bay leaves**
2 **tablespoons dried minced onion**
1 **tablespoon dried parsley flakes**
2 **teaspoons beef bouillon granules**
1 **teaspoon dried minced garlic**
1 **teaspoon dried thyme leaves**
½ **teaspoon dried oregano leaves**
½ **teaspoon black pepper**
¼ **teaspoon red pepper flakes**

1. Layer baby lima beans, kidney beans, Great Northern beans, red beans, navy beans and pinto beans in 1-quart food storage jar with tight-fitting lid. Slide bay leaves down side of jar. Place onion, parsley, bouillon granules, garlic, thyme, oregano, black pepper and red pepper flakes in small food storage bag. Close bag with twist tie; cut off top of bag. Place bag on top of beans. Close jar.

2. Cover top of jar with fabric; attach gift tag with recipe below.

Makes one 1-quart jar

Country Six Bean Soup

1 **jar Country Six Bean Soup Mix**
4 **to 5 cups water**
1 **can (28 ounces) diced tomatoes with Italian seasonings**
2 **smoked ham hocks** *or* 8 **ounces smoked sausage links, sliced**
   Hot pepper sauce or red wine vinegar (optional)

1. Remove seasoning packet and bay leaves; set aside.

2. Place beans in large bowl; cover with water. Soak 6 to 8 hours or overnight. (To quick-soak beans, place beans in large saucepan; cover with water. Bring to a boil over high heat. Boil 2 minutes. Remove from heat; let soak, covered, 1 hour.) Drain beans; discard water.

continued on page 64

Country Six Bean Soup

1 jar Country Six Bean Soup Mix
4 1/2 cups water
2 smoked ham hocks or 8 ounces
  smoked sausage links
1 can (28-ounces) diced tomatoes
  with Italian seasonings
Hot pepper sauce or red wine
  vinegar (optional)

1. Remove seasoning packet and bay leaves; set aside.
2. Place beans in large bowl; cover with water. (To quick soak beans, place beans in large saucepan; cover with water. Boil 2 minutes. Remove from heat; let soak. Soak 6 to 8 hours overnight. (To heat and water.
3. Combine soaked beans, water, tomatoes, ham hocks, contents of seasoning packet and reserved bay leaves in Dutch oven. Bring to a boil over high heat. Cover; reduce heat and simmer 1/2 to 2 hours or until beans are tender. Take out ham hocks; remove skin and cut meat from bones and pieces. Return meat to pan. Drain

Makes 8 to 10 servings

Country Six Bean Soup

3. Combine soaked beans, 4 cups water, tomatoes, ham hocks, contents of seasoning packet and reserved bay leaves in Dutch oven. Bring to a boil over high heat. Cover; reduce heat and simmer 1½ to 2 hours or until beans are tender, adding more water if necessary. Remove and discard bay leaves. Take out ham hocks; remove skin and cut meat from bones into pieces. Return meat to pan. Season to taste with hot pepper sauce, if desired.

Makes 8 to 10 servings

Note: For thicker consistency, mash beans slightly with potato masher.

Hot & Spicy Mustard

¼ **cup water**
¼ **cup whole yellow mustard seeds**
¼ **cup honey**
3 **tablespoons cider vinegar**
2 **tablespoons ground mustard**
1 **teaspoon salt**
⅛ **teaspoon ground cloves**

1. Place water in small saucepan. Bring to a boil over high heat. Add mustard seeds. Cover saucepan; remove from heat. Let stand 1 hour or until liquid is absorbed.

2. Combine mustard seeds, honey, vinegar, ground mustard, salt and cloves in food processor; process using on/off pulsing action until mixture is thickened and seeds are coarsely chopped, scraping down side of work bowl once. Refrigerate at least 1 day before serving. Store in airtight container in refrigerator up to 3 weeks.

Makes about 1 cup mustard

Cranberry-Orange Relish

4 large oranges, divided
7 (½-pint) jelly jars with lids and screw bands
2 cups sugar
½ cup water
2 packages (12 ounces each) fresh cranberries, washed and drained

1. Remove peel from 2 oranges in long strips with sharp paring knife, making sure there is no white pith on peel. Stack strips; cut into thin slivers. Measure ¼ cup; set aside.

2. Add orange peel to 1 inch boiling water in 1-quart saucepan. Boil over medium heat 5 minutes. Drain; set aside. Peel remaining 2 oranges; discard peel. Remove white pith from all 4 oranges; discard pith. Separate oranges into sections. With fingers, remove pulp from membrane of each section over 2-cup measure to save juice, discarding membrane. Dice orange sections into same cup. Add additional water to orange mixture to make 2 cups, if necessary; set aside.

3. Wash jars, lids and bands. Leave jars in hot water. Place lids and bands in large pan of water.

4. Combine sugar and water in heavy 6-quart saucepan or Dutch oven. Bring to a boil over medium heat. Add reserved orange peel, orange mixture and cranberries. Bring to a boil, stirring occasionally. Boil about 10 minutes or until mixture thickens and cranberries pop.

5. Bring water with lids and bands to a boil. Ladle hot mixture into hot jars, leaving ½-inch space at top. Run metal spatula around inside of jar to remove air bubbles. Wipe tops and sides of jar rims clean. Place hot lids and bands on jars. Screw bands tightly, but do not force. To process, place jars in boiling water; boil 10 minutes. Remove jars with tongs; cool on wire racks. (Check seals by pressing on lid with fingertip; lid should remain concave.) Label and date jars. Store unopened jars in cool, dry place up to 12 months. Refrigerate up to 6 months after opening. *Makes about seven ½-pint jars*

Chinese Mixed Pickled Vegetables

Pickling Liquid
- 3 cups sugar
- 3 cups distilled white vinegar
- 1½ cups water
- 1½ teaspoons salt

Vegetables
- 1 large Chinese white radish (about 1 pound), cut into matchstick pieces
- 3 large carrots, cut into matchstick pieces
- 1 large cucumber, seeded* and cut into matchstick pieces
- 4 ribs celery, diagonally cut into ½-inch pieces
- 8 green onions, diagonally cut into ¼-inch pieces
- 1 large red bell pepper, cut into ½-inch pieces
- 1 large green bell pepper, cut into ½-inch pieces
- 4 ounces fresh ginger, peeled and thinly sliced

Cut cucumber in half lengthwise; remove seeds with spoon.

1. Combine all pickling liquid ingredients in 3-quart saucepan. Bring to a boil over medium heat, stirring occasionally. Set aside and let cool.

2. Fill 5-quart stockpot or Dutch oven ½ full with water. Bring to a boil. Add all vegetables. Remove from heat. Let stand 2 minutes.

3. Drain vegetables in large colander. Spread vegetables out on clean towels; allow to dry 2 to 3 hours.

4. Pack vegetables firmly into clean jars with tight-fitting lids. Pour Pickling Liquid into jars to cover vegetables. Seal jars tightly. Store in refrigerator at least 1 week before using.   *Makes 1½ to 2 quarts vegetables*

Apricot Butter

- 1 cup dried apricots (5 ounces)
- 1 cup unsweetened apple juice

1. Combine apricots and juice in small saucepan; bring to a boil over medium-high heat. Reduce heat to low; cover and simmer 20 minutes, stirring occasionally. Remove from heat; cool slightly.

2. Pour mixture into blender or food processor; process until smooth. Cool to room temperature and refrigerate in airtight container or jar with tight fitting lid up to 3 months.   *Makes 16 servings*

Chinese Mixed Pickled Vegetables

Twelve Carat Black-Eyed Pea Relish

12 small carrots, peeled
1 cup vinegar
¼ cup vegetable oil
2 cans (15 ounces each) black-eyed peas, drained
1 sweet onion, chopped
1 green bell pepper, finely chopped
1 cup sugar
¼ cup Worcestershire sauce
2 teaspoons black pepper
2 teaspoons salt (optional)
2 dashes ground red pepper
   Fresh basil leaves for garnish

1. To steam carrots, place half the carrots in folding metal steamer or colander. Place steamer over a few inches of water in 2- or 3-quart saucepan with tight-fitting lid. (Be sure steamer is at least 1 inch above water.) Bring water to a boil; steam carrots until crisp-tender, 16 to 18 minutes, adding more water to saucepan if necessary to prevent saucepan from boiling dry. Carefully remove carrots from steamer; repeat with remaining carrots. Coarsely chop cooled carrots. Set aside.

2. Combine vinegar and oil in small saucepan. Bring to a boil.

3. Combine black-eyed peas, carrots, onion, bell pepper, sugar, Worcestershire sauce, black pepper, salt and ground red pepper in large bowl.

4. Pour oil mixture over vegetable mixture.

5. Marinate, covered, in refrigerator at least 24 hours. Store, covered, in clean glass jars in refrigerator. Serve cold. Garnish, if desired.

Makes 2 to 3 pints relish

Twelve Carat Black-Eyed Pea Relish

Way-Out Western BBQ Sauce

½ **cup chili sauce**
¼ **cup fresh lemon juice**
¼ **cup ketchup**
2 **tablespoons dry mustard**
2 **tablespoons brown sugar**
2 **tablespoons cider vinegar**
2 **tablespoons dark molasses**
1 **tablespoon Worcestershire sauce**
2 **teaspoons grated fresh lemon peel**
½ **teaspoon garlic powder**
½ **teaspoon ground allspice**
½ **teaspoon liquid smoke (optional)**
¼ **teaspoon hot pepper sauce**

1. Place all ingredients in small bowl and stir until blended.

2. Brush on meats during last 15 minutes of grilling or at beginning of grilling if cooking time is less than 15 minutes. *Makes 10 servings*

Note: To avoid spreading bacteria from raw meats with the basting brush, pour only the sauce needed for basting into a small bowl and discard any that remains after basting.

Classic Salsa

4 **medium tomatoes**
1 **small onion, finely chopped**
2 **to 3 jalapeño peppers or serrano peppers,* seeded and minced**
¼ **cup chopped fresh cilantro**
1 **small clove garlic, minced**
2 **tablespoons lime juice**
    Salt and black pepper to taste

*Jalapeño and serrano peppers can sting and irritate the skin; wear rubber gloves when handling peppers and do not touch eyes. Wash hands after handling.

1. Cut tomatoes in half; remove seeds. Coarsely chop tomatoes.

2. Combine tomatoes, onion, jalapeño peppers, cilantro, garlic and lime juice in medium bowl. Add salt and black pepper. Cover and refrigerate 1 hour or up to 3 days for flavors to blend. *Makes about 2½ cups salsa*

Way-Out Western BBQ Sauce

Bean Dip for a Crowd Mix

1½ cups dried black beans
1½ cups dried pinto beans
  2 bay leaves
  1 package (about 1¼ ounces) hot taco seasoning mix
  2 tablespoons dried minced onion
  3 chicken bouillon cubes, unwrapped
  1 tablespoon dried parsley flakes

1. Layer black beans and pinto beans in 1-quart food storage jar with tight-fitting lid. Slide bay leaves down side of jar. Place taco seasoning, onion, bouillon cubes and parsley in small food storage bag. Close bag with twist tie and cut off top of bag. Place bag on top of beans. Close jar.

2. Cover top of jar with fabric; attach gift tag with recipe below.

Makes one 1-quart jar

Bean Dip for a Crowd

  1 jar Bean Dip for a Crowd Mix
  5 cups water
  1 jar (16 ounces) thick and chunky salsa (medium or hot)
  2 tablespoons lime juice

1. Remove seasoning packet and bay leaves from jar; set aside.

2. Place beans in large bowl; cover with water. Soak 6 to 8 hours or overnight. (To quick-soak beans, place beans in large saucepan; cover with water. Bring to a boil over high heat. Boil 2 minutes. Remove from heat; let soak, covered, 1 hour.) Drain beans; discard water.

3. Combine soaked beans, water, contents of seasoning packet and bay leaves in slow cooker. Cover and cook on LOW 9 to 10 hours or until beans are tender. Add additional water, ½ cup at a time, if needed. Remove and discard bay leaves.

4. Ladle ½ hot bean mixture into food processor. Add salsa and lime juice. Cover and process until smooth. Return puréed dip to slow cooker; stir to combine.

Makes 6 cups dip

Conventional Method: Simmer bean mixture in step 3 in Dutch oven, partially covered, 2½ hours or until tender. Continue as directed in step 4.

Gift Idea: Assemble a gift basket with a jar of Bean Dip for a Crowd, salsa, fresh limes and tortilla chips.

Bean Dip for a Crowd

Apple-Cheddar Scones

1 recipe Apple-Cheddar Scone Mix (recipe follows)
6 tablespoons cold butter, cut into pieces
1 apple, peeled, cored and chopped
½ cup plus 2 tablespoons shredded Cheddar cheese, divided
½ cup water

1. Preheat oven to 400°F. Lightly grease large baking sheet. Set aside.

2. Pour scone mix into large bowl. Cut in butter with pastry blender until mixture resembles coarse crumbs. Stir in apple and ½ cup cheese. Stir in water until soft dough forms; form into ball.

3. Place dough on prepared baking sheet. Press into 8-inch round with lightly floured hands. Cut into 8 wedges with lightly floured knife; slightly separate pieces by moving knife back and forth between slices. Sprinkle remaining 2 tablespoons cheese evenly over wedges.

4. Bake 20 minutes or until lightly browned. Remove scones to wire rack; cool completely. Store in airtight container at room temperature up to 3 days.

Makes 8 scones

Apple-Cheddar Scone Mix

1¾ cups all-purpose flour
2 tablespoons powdered buttermilk
1 tablespoon sugar
1 teaspoon baking powder
¾ teaspoon dried thyme leaves
¼ teaspoon baking soda
¼ teaspoon salt

Combine all ingredients in small bowl until well blended. Store in airtight container at room temperature up to 3 months.　　*Makes about 2 cups mix*

Pear Pepper Relish

3 pounds Northwest Bartlett pears, pared, cored and chopped
2 green peppers, seeded and chopped
2 red peppers, seeded and chopped
1½ cups chopped onion
1 can (4 ounces) diced chiles
1½ cups cider vinegar
¾ cup sugar
1½ teaspoons salt
½ teaspoon ground cinnamon
½ teaspoon ground cloves

Combine all ingredients in large Dutch oven. Bring to a boil; reduce heat and simmer about 1 hour or until thickened. Stir occasionally as mixture thickens. Remove from heat; ladle into clean hot canning jars to within ⅛ inch of tops. Seal according to jar manufacturer's directions.

Place jars on rack in canner. Process 10 minutes in boiling water bath with boiling water two inches above jar tops. Remove jars from canner. Place on thick cloth or racks; cool away from drafts.

After 12 hours test lids for proper seal; remove rings from sealed jars.

Makes 3 pints relish

Favorite recipe from **Pear Bureau Northwest**

Basil Garlic Vinegar

½ cup coarsely chopped fresh basil leaves
2 cloves garlic, peeled and split
1 bottle (16 ounces) HEINZ® Wine or Distilled White Vinegar
Fresh basil leaves, for garnish

Place chopped basil and garlic in sterilized pint jar. Heat vinegar to *just* below boiling point. Fill jar with vinegar and seal tightly. Allow to stand 3 to 4 weeks. Strain vinegar, discarding basil and garlic. Pour vinegar into clean sterilized jar, adding basil leaves for garnish, if desired. Seal tightly. Use in dressings for rice, pasta, salads or in mayonnaise.

Makes 2 cups vinegar

Breads & Muffins

Grandma's® Bran Muffins

2½ cups bran flakes, divided
1 cup raisins
1 cup boiling water
2 cups buttermilk
1 cup GRANDMA'S® Molasses
½ cup canola oil
2 eggs, beaten
2¾ cups all-purpose flour
2½ teaspoons baking soda
½ teaspoon salt

Heat oven to 400°F. In medium bowl, mix 1 cup bran flakes, raisins and water. Set aside. In large bowl, combine remaining ingredients. Mix in bran-raisin mixture. Pour into greased muffin pan cups. Fill ⅔ full and bake for 20 minutes. Remove muffins and place on rack to cool.   *Makes 48 muffins*

 gift tip

Celebrate a birthday, anniversary or even a new job with a "Good Morning" gift basket. Include these muffins, some flavored coffees and a set of mugs. It's sure to start the day off with a smile!

Grandma's® Bran Muffins

Orange Marmalade Bread

3 cups all-purpose flour
4 teaspoons baking powder
1 teaspoon salt
½ cup chopped walnuts
¾ cup milk
¾ cup SMUCKER'S® Orange Marmalade
2 eggs, lightly beaten
¼ cup honey
2 tablespoons oil

Grease 9×5×3-inch loaf pan. Combine flour, baking powder and salt in large bowl. Stir in nuts. Combine milk, marmalade, eggs, honey and oil; blend well. Add to flour mixture; stir only until dry ingredients are moistened (batter will be lumpy). Turn into prepared pan.

Bake at 350°F for 65 to 70 minutes or until lightly browned and toothpick inserted in center comes out clean.   *Makes 8 to 10 servings*

Touchdown Cheese Scones

2 cups all-purpose flour
2½ teaspoons baking powder
½ teaspoon baking soda
¼ teaspoon salt
2 tablespoons cold butter or margarine, cut in pieces
1 cup shredded mild Cheddar cheese
⅔ cup buttermilk
2 eggs
½ teaspoon TABASCO® brand Pepper Sauce

Preheat oven to 350°F. Sift together flour, baking powder, baking soda and salt in large bowl. Cut in butter until mixture resembles cornmeal. Stir in cheese. Blend buttermilk, 1 egg and TABASCO® Sauce together in small bowl. Make a well in center of dry ingredients; add buttermilk mixture. Stir quickly and lightly with fork to form sticky dough. Turn dough out on lightly floured board. Knead gently 10 times. Divide dough in half; pat each half into circle about ½ inch thick. Cut each circle into 4 wedges. Combine remaining egg and 1 tablespoon water. Brush each wedge with egg mixture. Arrange on greased baking sheet. Bake 13 to 15 minutes or until golden.   *Makes 8 scones*

Orange Marmalade Bread

Peanut Butter Mini Muffins

⅓ cup creamy peanut butter
¼ cup (½ stick) butter, softened
¼ cup granulated sugar
¼ cup firmly packed light brown sugar
 1 egg
¾ cup buttermilk
 3 tablespoons vegetable oil
¾ teaspoon vanilla extract
1½ cups all-purpose flour
¾ teaspoon baking powder
½ teaspoon baking soda
½ teaspoon salt
1¼ cups "M&M's"® Milk Chocolate Mini Baking Bits, divided
   Chocolate Glaze (recipe follows)

Preheat oven to 350°F. Lightly grease 36 (1¾-inch) mini muffin cups or line with paper or foil liners; set aside. In large bowl cream peanut butter, butter and sugars until light and fluffy; beat in egg. Beat in buttermilk, oil and vanilla. In medium bowl combine flour, baking powder, baking soda and salt; gradually blend into creamed mixture. Divide batter evenly among prepared muffin cups. Sprinkle batter evenly with ¾ cup "M&M's"® Milk Chocolate Mini Baking Bits. Bake 15 to 17 minutes or until toothpick inserted in centers comes out clean. Cool completely on wire racks. Prepare Chocolate Glaze. Place glaze in resealable plastic sandwich bag; seal bag. Cut tiny piece off one corner of bag (not more than ⅛ inch). Drizzle glaze over muffins. Decorate with remaining ½ cup "M&M's"® Milk Chocolate Mini Baking Bits; let glaze set. Store in tightly covered container.   *Makes 3 dozen mini muffins*

Chocolate Glaze: In top of double boiler over hot water melt 2 (1-ounce) squares semi-sweet chocolate and 1 tablespoon butter. Stir until smooth; let cool slightly.

Peanut Butter Mini Muffins

Chocolate Chip Coffeecake

   3 cups all-purpose flour
⅓ cup sugar
   2 envelopes FLEISCHMANN'S® RapidRise™ Yeast
   1 teaspoon salt
½ cup milk
½ cup water
½ cup butter or margarine
   2 eggs
¾ cup semi-sweet chocolate morsels
   Chocolate Nut Topping (recipe follows)

In large bowl, combine 1 cup flour, sugar, undissolved yeast and salt. Heat milk, water and butter until very warm (120° to 130°F). Gradually add to dry ingredients. Beat 2 minutes at medium speed of electric mixer, scraping bowl occasionally. Add eggs and 1 cup flour; beat 2 minutes at high speed, scraping bowl occasionally. Stir in chocolate morsels and remaining flour to make a soft batter. Turn into greased 13×9×2-inch baking pan. Cover; let rise in warm, draft-free place until doubled in size, about 1 hour.

Bake at 400°F for 15 minutes; remove from oven and sprinkle with Chocolate Nut Topping. Return to oven and bake additional 10 minutes or until done. Cool in pan for 10 minutes. Remove from pan; cool on wire rack.

Makes 1 cake

Chocolate Nut Topping: In medium bowl, cut ½ cup butter into ⅔ cup all-purpose flour until crumbly. Stir in ⅔ cup sugar, 2 teaspoons ground cinnamon, 1 cup semi-sweet chocolate morsels and 1 cup chopped pecans.

Chocolate Chip Coffeecake

Heavenly Lemon Muffins

1 (16-ounce) package angel food cake mix
3 cups all-purpose flour
4 teaspoons baking powder
½ teaspoon salt
1 cup granulated sugar
⅔ cup skim milk
⅔ cup MOTT'S® Natural Apple Sauce
¼ cup vegetable oil
2 egg whites
2 tablespoons grated lemon peel
2 teaspoons lemon extract
4 drops yellow food coloring (optional)
2 tablespoons powdered sugar (optional)

1. Preheat oven to 375°F. Line 24 (2½-inch) muffin cups with paper liners or spray with nonstick cooking spray.

2. In large bowl, prepare angel food cake mix according to package directions.

3. In another large bowl, combine flour, baking powder and salt.

4. In medium bowl, combine granulated sugar, milk, apple sauce, oil, egg whites, lemon peel, lemon extract and food coloring, if desired.

5. Stir apple sauce mixture into flour mixture just until moistened.

6. Fill each muffin cup ⅓ full with apple sauce batter. Top with angel food cake batter, filling each cup almost full.*

7. Bake 20 minutes or until golden and puffed. Immediately remove from pan; cool completely on wire rack. Sprinkle tops with powdered sugar, if desired.

Makes 24 servings

*There will be some angel food cake batter remaining.

Heavenly Strawberry Muffins: Substitute strawberry extract for lemon extract and red food coloring for yellow food coloring, if desired. Omit lemon peel.

Heavenly Lemon Muffins
and Heavenly Strawberry Muffin

Soft Pretzels

1 package (16 ounces) hot roll mix plus ingredients to prepare mix
1 egg white
2 teaspoons water
2 tablespoons *each* assorted coatings: coarse salt, sesame seeds, poppy seeds, dried oregano leaves

1. Prepare hot roll mix according to package directions.

2. Preheat oven to 375°F. Spray baking sheets with nonstick cooking spray; set aside.

3. Divide dough equally into 16 pieces; roll each piece with hands to form rope, 7 to 10 inches long. Place on prepared cookie sheets; form into desired shape (hearts, wreaths, pretzels, snails, loops, etc.).

4. Beat egg white and water in small bowl until foamy. Brush onto dough shapes; sprinkle each shape with 1½ teaspoons of one coating.

5. Bake until golden brown, about 15 minutes. Serve warm or at room temperature.

Makes 8 servings

Apricot-Peanut Butter Muffins

1¾ cups all-purpose flour
2½ tablespoons sugar
2½ teaspoons baking powder
¾ teaspoon salt
¼ cup shortening
¼ cup SMUCKER'S® Creamy Natural Peanut Butter
1 egg, well beaten
¾ cup milk
2 tablespoons SMUCKER'S® Apricot Preserves

Grease 10 large muffin cups. Combine flour, sugar, baking powder and salt; cut in shortening and peanut butter. Mix egg and milk together and add all at once to dry ingredients. Stir only until dry ingredients are moistened. Fill muffin cups ⅔ full. Spoon about ½ teaspoon preserves in center of each muffin.

Bake at 400°F for 25 minutes or until done.

Makes 10 muffins

Soft Pretzels

Coconut Chocolate Chip Loaf

1 package DUNCAN HINES® Bakery-Style Chocolate Chip Muffin Mix
1⅓ cups toasted flaked coconut (see Note)
¾ cup water
1 egg
½ teaspoon vanilla extract
    Confectioners' sugar for garnish (optional)

1. Preheat oven to 350°F. Grease and flour 9×5×3-inch loaf pan.

2. Empty muffin mix into medium bowl. Break up any lumps. Add coconut, water, egg and vanilla extract. Stir until moistened, about 50 strokes. Pour into prepared pan. Bake at 350°F for 45 to 50 minutes or until toothpick inserted in center comes out clean. Cool in pan 15 minutes. Invert onto cooling rack. Turn right side up. Cool completely. Dust with confectioners' sugar, if desired.

Makes 1 loaf (12 slices)

Note: Spread coconut evenly on baking sheet. Toast at 350°F for 5 minutes. Stir and toast 1 to 2 minutes longer or until light golden brown.

Irish Soda Bread

    4 cups sifted all-purpose flour
    1 tablespoon sugar
1½ teaspoons ARM & HAMMER® Baking Soda
    1 teaspoon baking powder
    ½ teaspoon salt
    ¼ cup unsalted margarine or butter-flavored hydrogenated shortening
    1 cup seedless raisins
1½ cups buttermilk

Sift together flour, sugar, Baking Soda, baking powder and salt into large bowl. Cut in margarine until crumbly. Stir in raisins. Add buttermilk and stir to make a soft dough. Turn onto lightly floured board and knead to form a smooth ball.

Place dough on greased baking sheet; pat with hands to 1¼-inch thickness. With sharp knife score dough into 4 sections. Bake in 350°F oven 1 hour or until bread is browned and toothpick inserted in center comes out clean. Serve warm with butter.

Makes 1 loaf

Coconut Chocolate Chip Loaf

Nutty Lemon Bread

PAM® No-Stick Cooking Spray

Bread
- 2 cups all-purpose flour
- 2 teaspoons baking powder
- ¾ teaspoon salt
- 1½ cups sugar
- ¾ cup WESSON® Canola or Vegetable Oil
- 3 eggs
- 3 tablespoons grated fresh lemon peel
- 1 teaspoon vanilla
- ¾ cup milk
- ½ cup finely chopped pecans

Glaze
- 1 cup sifted powdered sugar
- 1 tablespoon orange juice
- 1 teaspoon grated fresh lemon peel

Preheat oven to 350°F. Spray two 8×4×2½-inch loaf pans with PAM Cooking Spray; lightly dust with flour.

Bread

In a medium bowl, sift together flour, baking powder and salt. In a large mixing bowl, combine sugar, Wesson Oil, eggs, lemon peel and vanilla. On LOW speed, beat mixture for 2 minutes. Continue mixing while alternately adding dry ingredients and milk to egg mixture; blend well. Fold in nuts. Evenly divide batter into loaf pans. Bake 40 to 50 minutes or until wooden pick inserted into centers comes out clean. Cool on wire racks 10 minutes. Run knife around bread to loosen sides. Remove bread from pans and cool completely.

Glaze

While bread is cooling, combine *all* glaze ingredients. Mix until sugar is completely dissolved and glaze is smooth. Spoon glaze evenly over bread allowing glaze to drip.

Makes 2 loaves

Pumpkin Apple Streusel Muffins

Muffins
 2½ cups all-purpose flour
   2 cups granulated sugar
   1 tablespoon pumpkin pie spice
   1 teaspoon baking soda
   ½ teaspoon salt
 1¼ cups LIBBY'S® 100% Pure Pumpkin
   2 eggs
   ¼ cup vegetable oil
   2 cups peeled, cored and finely chopped apples (2 small)

Streusel Topping
   ¼ cup granulated sugar
   2 tablespoons all-purpose flour
   ½ teaspoon ground cinnamon
   2 tablespoons butter or margarine

For Muffins
PREHEAT oven to 350°F. Grease or paper-line 18 muffin cups.

COMBINE flour, sugar, pumpkin pie spice, baking soda and salt in large bowl. Combine pumpkin, eggs and vegetable oil in medium bowl; mix well. Stir into flour mixture just until moistened. Stir in apples. Spoon batter into prepared muffin cups, filling ¾ full.

For Streusel Topping
COMBINE sugar, flour and cinnamon in medium bowl. Cut in butter with pastry blender or two knives until mixture is crumbly. Sprinkle over muffin batter.

BAKE for 30 to 35 minutes or until wooden pick inserted in centers comes out clean. Cool in pans for 5 minutes; remove to wire racks to cool slightly.

Makes 18 muffins

Calico Bell Pepper Muffins

¼ cup finely chopped red bell pepper
¼ cup finely chopped yellow bell pepper
¼ cup finely chopped green bell pepper
2 tablespoons margarine
2 cups all-purpose flour
4 tablespoons sugar
1 tablespoon baking powder
¾ teaspoon salt
½ teaspoon dried basil leaves
1 cup low-fat milk
1 whole egg
2 egg whites

Preheat oven to 400°F. Paper-line 12 muffin cups or spray with cooking spray. In small skillet, cook peppers in margarine over medium-high heat until color is bright and peppers are tender-crisp, about 3 minutes. Set aside.

In large bowl, combine flour, sugar, baking powder, salt and basil. In small bowl, combine milk, whole egg and egg whites until blended. Add milk mixture and peppers with drippings to flour mixture and stir until just moistened. Spoon into prepared muffin cups. Bake 15 minutes or until golden and wooden pick inserted in centers comes out clean. Cool briefly and remove from pan. *Makes 12 muffins*

Favorite recipe from **The Sugar Association, Inc.**

Calico Bell Pepper Muffins

Cranberry Oat Bread

¾ cup honey
⅓ cup vegetable oil
2 eggs
½ cup milk
2½ cups all-purpose flour
1 cup quick-cooking rolled oats
1 teaspoon baking soda
1 teaspoon baking powder
½ teaspoon salt
½ teaspoon ground cinnamon
2 cups fresh or frozen cranberries
1 cup chopped nuts

Combine honey, oil, eggs and milk in large bowl; mix well. Combine flour, oats, baking soda, baking powder, salt and cinnamon in medium bowl; mix well. Stir into honey mixture. Fold in cranberries and nuts. Spoon into two 8½×4½×2½-inch greased and floured loaf pans.

Bake in preheated 350°F oven 40 to 45 minutes or until wooden toothpick inserted near centers comes out clean. Cool in pans on wire racks 15 minutes. Remove from pans; cool completely on wire racks.   *Makes 2 loaves*

Favorite recipe from **National Honey Board**

gift tip

A loaf of this hearty bread makes a great house-warming gift. Wrap the cooled bread in plastic wrap and place it in a new loaf pan. Add some measuring spoons or a rubber scraper and then wrap it all up in a colorful kitchen towel.

Cranberry Oat Bread

Chunky Apple Molasses Muffins

2 cups all-purpose flour
¼ cup sugar
1 tablespoon baking powder
1 teaspoon ground cinnamon
¼ teaspoon salt
1 Fuji apple, peeled, cored and finely chopped
½ cup milk
¼ cup vegetable oil
¼ cup molasses
1 egg

1. Heat oven to 450°F. Lightly grease eight 3-inch muffin pan cups. In large bowl, combine flour, sugar, baking powder, cinnamon and salt. Add apple and stir to distribute evenly.

2. In small bowl, beat together milk, oil, molasses and egg. Stir into dry ingredients and mix just until blended. Fill muffin pan cups with batter. Bake 5 minutes. *Reduce heat to 350°F* and bake 12 to 15 minutes longer or until centers of muffins spring back when gently pressed. Cool in pan 5 minutes. Remove muffins from pan and cool slightly; serve warm.

Makes 8 (3-inch) muffins

Favorite recipe from **Washington Apple Commission**

Chunky Apple Molasses Muffins

Pumpkin-Pecan Friendship Bread

3 cups chopped pecans, divided
1 can (16 ounces) solid-pack pumpkin
1 cup Starter (recipe follows)
4 eggs
½ cup vegetable oil
2 teaspoons vanilla
3 cups all-purpose flour
1 cup granulated sugar
1 cup packed light brown sugar
4 teaspoons ground cinnamon
2 teaspoons baking powder
1 teaspoon baking soda
1 teaspoon ground nutmeg
1 teaspoon ground ginger
1 teaspoon ground cloves

1. Preheat oven to 350°F. Grease and flour 2 (9½×4-inch) loaf pans. Set aside.

2. Reserve 1 cup pecans. Spread remaining 2 cups pecans in single layer in large baking pan. Bake 8 minutes or until golden brown, stirring frequently.

3. Combine pumpkin, 1 cup Starter, eggs, oil and vanilla in large bowl. Combine remaining ingredients in separate large bowl until well blended. Stir into pumpkin mixture just until blended. Stir in toasted pecans. Spoon batter evenly into prepared pans. Sprinkle reserved pecans evenly over batter.

4. Bake 1 hour or until wooden pick inserted in centers comes out clean. Cool in pans on wire rack 5 minutes. Remove from pans. Cool completely on wire rack. Wrap in plastic wrap. Store at room temperature up to 1 week.

Makes 2 loaves

Starter

1 cup sugar
1 cup all-purpose flour
1 cup milk

1. Combine all ingredients in large resealable plastic food storage bag. Knead bag until well blended. Let bag stand at room temperature 5 days. Knead bag 5 times each day.

continued on page 100

Pumpkin-Pecan Friendship Bread

2. On day 6, add 1 cup sugar, 1 cup flour and 1 cup milk. Knead bag until well blended. Let stand at room temperature 4 days. Knead bag 5 times each day.

3. On day 10, pour 1 cup Starter into each of 3 bags. Reserve remaining 1 cup Starter for recipe. Give remaining bags of Starter with recipe as gifts.

Makes about 4 cups starter

Banana Chocolate Chip Muffins
Prep Time: *20 minutes* • **Bake Time:** *30 minutes*

 2 ripe, medium DOLE® Bananas
 1 cup packed brown sugar
 2 eggs
 ½ cup margarine, melted
 1 teaspoon vanilla extract
2¼ cups all-purpose flour
 2 teaspoons baking powder
 ½ teaspoon ground cinnamon
 ½ teaspoon salt
 1 cup chocolate chips
 ½ cup chopped walnuts

• Purée bananas in blender (1 cup). Beat bananas, sugar, eggs, margarine and vanilla in medium bowl until well blended.

• Combine flour, baking powder, cinnamon and salt in large bowl. Stir in chocolate chips and nuts. Make well in center of dry ingredients. Add banana mixture. Stir just until blended. Spoon into well greased 2½-inch muffin pan cups.

• Bake at 350°F 25 to 30 minutes or until toothpick inserted in centers comes out clean. Cool slightly; remove from pan and place on wire rack.

Makes 12 muffins

Petit Pain au Chocolate

3 to 3½ cups all-purpose flour
3 tablespoons granulated sugar
1 package (¼ ounce) active dry yeast
1 teaspoon salt
1 cup plus 1 tablespoon milk, divided
3 tablespoons butter or margarine, at room temperature
1 egg, lightly beaten
1 milk chocolate candy bar (7 ounces), cut into 16 pieces
2 teaspoons colored sugar

1. Combine 3 cups flour, granulated sugar, yeast and salt in large bowl; set aside.

2. Combine 1 cup milk and butter in small saucepan. Heat over low heat until mixture is 120° to 130°F. (Butter does not need to completely melt.)

3. Gradually stir milk mixture and egg into flour mixture to make soft dough that forms ball.

4. Turn out dough onto lightly floured surface; flatten slightly. Knead dough 8 to 10 minutes or until smooth and elastic, adding remaining ½ cup flour to prevent sticking if necessary.

5. Shape dough into ball; place in large greased bowl. Turn dough over so that top is greased. Cover with towel; let rise in warm place about 1 hour or until doubled in bulk.

6. Punch down dough. Knead dough on lightly floured surface 1 minute. Roll dough back and forth, forming loaf.

7. Cut loaf into 8 pieces. Roll 1 dough piece into 6-inch round. Place 2 pieces chocolate in center. Fold edges into center around chocolate. Place seam side down on lightly greased baking sheet. Repeat with remaining dough pieces. Place rolls 3 inches apart on baking sheet.

8. Cover rolls lightly with towel and let rise in warm place 20 to 30 minutes or until slightly puffed. Brush tops with remaining 1 tablespoon milk. Sprinkle with colored sugar.

9. Preheat oven to 400°F. Bake 12 to 15 minutes or until rolls are golden brown. Serve immediately. *Makes 8 rolls*

Brunchtime Sour Cream Cupcakes

1 cup (2 sticks) butter, softened
2 cups plus 4 teaspoons sugar, divided
2 eggs
1 cup sour cream
1 teaspoon almond extract
2 cups all-purpose flour
1 teaspoon salt
½ teaspoon baking soda
1 cup chopped walnuts
1½ teaspoons ground cinnamon
⅛ teaspoon nutmeg

1. Preheat oven to 350°F. Insert paper liners into 18 muffin cups.

2. Beat butter and 2 cups sugar in large bowl. Add eggs, one at a time, beating well after each addition. Blend in sour cream and almond extract.

3. Combine flour, salt and baking soda in medium bowl. Add to butter mixture; mix well.

4. Stir together remaining 4 teaspoons sugar, walnuts, cinnamon and nutmeg in small bowl.

5. Fill prepared muffin cups ⅓ full with batter; sprinkle with ⅔ of the walnut mixture. Cover with remaining batter. Sprinkle with remaining walnut mixture.

6. Bake 25 to 30 minutes or until wooden toothpick inserted into centers comes out clean. Remove cupcakes from pan; cool on wire rack.

Makes 1½ dozen cupcakes

Brunchtime Sour Cream Cupcakes

Orange Cinnamon Swirl Bread

Bread
- 1 package DUNCAN HINES® Bakery-Style Cinnamon Swirl Muffin Mix
- 1 egg
- ⅔ cup orange juice
- 1 tablespoon grated orange peel

Orange Glaze
- ½ cup confectioners' sugar
- 2 to 3 teaspoons orange juice
- 1 teaspoon grated orange peel
- Quartered orange slices for garnish (optional)

1. Preheat oven to 350°F. Grease and flour 8½×4½×2½-inch loaf pan.

2. For bread, combine muffin mix and contents of topping packet from mix in large bowl. Break up any lumps. Add egg, ⅔ cup orange juice and 1 tablespoon orange peel. Stir until moistened, about 50 strokes. Knead swirl packet from mix for 10 seconds before opening. Squeeze contents on top of batter. Swirl into batter with knife or spatula, folding from bottom of bowl to get an even swirl. *Do not completely mix in.* Pour into prepared pan. Bake at 350°F for 55 to 60 minutes or until toothpick inserted in center comes out clean. Cool in pan 10 minutes. Loosen loaf from pan. Invert onto cooling rack. Turn right side up. Cool completely.

3. For orange glaze, place confectioners' sugar in small bowl. Add orange juice, 1 teaspoon at a time, stirring until smooth and of desired consistency. Stir in 1 teaspoon orange peel. Drizzle over loaf. Garnish with orange slices, if desired.

Makes 1 loaf (12 slices)

Note: If glaze becomes too thin, add more confectioners' sugar. If glaze is too thick, add more orange juice.

Orange Cinnamon Swirl Bread

Peach Gingerbread Muffins

2 cups all-purpose flour
2 teaspoons baking powder
1 teaspoon ground ginger
½ teaspoon salt
½ teaspoon ground cinnamon
¼ teaspoon ground cloves
½ cup sugar
½ cup MOTT'S® Chunky Apple Sauce
¼ cup MOTT'S® Apple Juice
¼ cup GRANDMA'S® Molasses
1 egg
2 tablespoons vegetable oil
1 (16-ounce) can peaches in juice, drained and chopped

1. Preheat oven to 400°F. Line 12 (2½-inch) muffin cups with paper liners or spray with nonstick cooking spray.

2. In large bowl, combine flour, baking powder, ginger, salt and spices.

3. In small bowl, combine sugar, apple sauce, apple juice, molasses, egg and oil.

4. Stir apple sauce mixture into flour mixture just until moistened. Fold in peaches.

5. Spoon batter evenly into prepared muffin cups.

6. Bake 20 minutes or until toothpick inserted in centers comes out clean. Immediately remove from pan; cool on wire rack 10 minutes. Serve warm or cool completely.   *Makes 12 servings*

Peach Gingerbread Muffins

Honey Currant Scones

2½ cups all-purpose flour
2 teaspoons grated orange peel
1 teaspoon baking powder
½ teaspoon baking soda
½ teaspoon salt
½ cup cold butter or margarine
½ cup currants
½ cup sour cream
⅓ cup honey
1 egg, slightly beaten

Preheat oven to 375°F. Grease baking sheet; set aside.

Combine flour, orange peel, baking powder, baking soda and salt in large bowl. Cut in butter with pastry blender or 2 knives until mixture resembles coarse crumbs. Add currants. Combine sour cream, honey and egg in medium bowl until well blended. Stir into flour mixture until soft dough forms. Turn out dough onto lightly floured surface. Knead dough 10 times. Shape dough into 8-inch square. Cut into 4 squares; cut each square diagonally in half, making 8 triangles. Place triangles 1 inch apart on prepared baking sheet.

Bake 15 to 20 minutes or until golden brown and wooden pick inserted in centers comes out clean. Remove from baking sheet. Cool on wire rack 10 minutes. Serve warm or cool completely.

Makes 8 scones

Favorite recipe from **National Honey Board**

gift tip

An assortment of teas, preserves, clotted cream and these scones would make a delicious "Tea Time" package. Look for clotted, or Devonshire, cream in the imported section of the supermarket or in specialty food shops.

Honey Currant Scones

Chocolate Streusel Pecan Muffins

Topping
- ¼ cup all-purpose flour
- ¼ cup packed brown sugar
- ¼ teaspoon ground cinnamon
- 2 tablespoons butter, melted
- ¼ cup chopped pecans

Muffins
- 1¾ cups (11.5-ounce package) NESTLÉ® TOLL HOUSE® Milk Chocolate Morsels, *divided*
- ⅓ cup milk
- 3 tablespoons butter
- 1 cup all-purpose flour
- 2 tablespoons granulated sugar
- 2 teaspoons baking powder
- ¼ teaspoon ground cinnamon
- ¾ cup chopped pecans
- 1 egg
- ½ teaspoon vanilla extract

For Topping

COMBINE flour, brown sugar, cinnamon and butter in small bowl with fork until mixture resembles coarse crumbs. Stir in nuts.

For Muffins

PREHEAT oven to 375°F. Grease or paper-line 12 muffin cups.

COMBINE *1 cup* morsels, milk and butter over hot (not boiling) water. Stir until morsels are melted and mixture is smooth.

COMBINE flour, granulated sugar, baking powder, cinnamon, pecans and *remaining* morsels in large bowl.

COMBINE egg, vanilla extract and melted morsel mixture in small bowl; stir into flour mixture just until moistened. Spoon into prepared muffin cups, filling ⅔ full. Sprinkle with topping.

BAKE for 20 to 25 minutes. Cool in pan for 5 minutes; remove to wire rack to cool completely.   *Makes 12 muffins*

Golden Cheddar Batter Bread

1 package active dry yeast
¾ cup warm water (110° to 115°F)
3 cups unsifted all-purpose flour, divided
1½ cups finely chopped Golden Delicious apples
1 cup shredded Cheddar cheese
2 eggs, lightly beaten
2 tablespoons vegetable shortening
2 tablespoons sugar
1 teaspoon salt
Buttery Apple Spread (recipe follows)

1. In large bowl, combine yeast and water, stirring to dissolve yeast. Set aside until mixture begins to foam, about 5 minutes. Add 1½ cups flour, apples, cheese, eggs, shortening, sugar and salt to yeast mixture; beat with electric mixer at medium speed 2 minutes. Beat in remaining flour gradually with spoon. Cover with clean cloth and let rise 50 to 60 minutes or until doubled. Meanwhile, prepare Buttery Apple Spread.

2. Grease 9×5-inch loaf pan. Beat batter by hand 30 seconds. Spread batter evenly in prepared pan. Cover with cloth and let rise 40 minutes or until nearly doubled.

3. Heat oven to 375°F. Bake bread 45 to 55 minutes or until loaf sounds hollow when gently tapped. Remove from pan; cool on wire rack at least 15 minutes. Serve with Buttery Apple Spread. *Makes 1 loaf*

Buttery Apple Spread: Peel, core and slice 1 Golden Delicious apple; place in small saucepan with 1 tablespoon water. Cover tightly and cook over medium heat until apple is very tender. Mash apple with fork; cool completely. In small bowl, beat ½ cup softened butter with electric mixer until light and fluffy. Gradually add mashed apple; beat until well combined. Makes about 1 cup.

Favorite recipe from **Washington Apple Commission**

All Kinds of Cookies

Black & White Hearts

¾ cup sugar
1 cup butter, softened
1 package (3 ounces) cream cheese, softened
1 egg
1½ teaspoons vanilla
3 cups all-purpose flour
1 cup semisweet chocolate chips
2 tablespoons shortening

1. Combine sugar, butter, cream cheese, egg and vanilla in large bowl. Beat at medium speed of electric mixer, scraping bowl often, until light and fluffy. Add flour; beat until well mixed. Divide dough in half; wrap each half in waxed paper. Refrigerate 2 hours or until firm.

2. Preheat oven to 375°F. Roll out dough to ⅛-inch thickness on lightly floured surface. Cut out with lightly floured 2-inch heart-shaped cookie cutter. Place 1 inch apart on ungreased cookie sheets. Bake 7 to 10 minutes or until edges are very lightly browned. Remove immediately to wire racks to cool completely.

3. Melt chocolate chips and shortening in small saucepan over low heat 4 to 6 minutes or until melted. Dip half of each heart into melted chocolate. Refrigerate on cookie sheets or trays lined with waxed paper until chocolate is firm. Store, covered, in refrigerator. *Makes about 3½ dozen cookies*

Black & White Hearts

Jumbo 3-Chip Cookies

   4 cups all-purpose flour
   1 teaspoon baking powder
   1 teaspoon baking soda
1½ cups (3 sticks) butter, softened
1¼ cups granulated sugar
1¼ cups packed brown sugar
   2 eggs
   1 tablespoon vanilla extract
   1 cup (6 ounces) NESTLÉ® TOLL HOUSE® Milk Chocolate Morsels
   1 cup (6 ounces) NESTLÉ® TOLL HOUSE® Semi-Sweet Chocolate Morsels
   ½ cup NESTLÉ® TOLL HOUSE® Premier White Morsels
   1 cup chopped nuts

PREHEAT oven to 375°F.

COMBINE flour, baking powder and baking soda in medium bowl. Beat butter, granulated sugar and brown sugar in large mixer bowl until creamy. Beat in eggs and vanilla extract. Gradually beat in flour mixture. Stir in morsels and nuts. Drop dough by level ¼-cup measure 2 inches apart onto ungreased baking sheets.

BAKE for 12 to 14 minutes or until light golden brown. Cool on baking sheets for 2 minutes; remove to wire racks to cool completely.

Makes about 2 dozen cookies

Chocolate Chip Macaroons

2½ cups flaked coconut
   ⅔ cup mini semisweet chocolate chips
   ⅔ cup sweetened condensed milk
   1 teaspoon vanilla

1. Preheat oven to 350°F. Grease cookie sheets. Combine coconut, chocolate chips, milk and vanilla in medium bowl; mix until well blended.

2. Drop dough by rounded teaspoonfuls 2 inches apart onto prepared cookie sheets. Press dough gently with back of spoon to flatten slightly. Bake 10 to 12 minutes or until light golden brown.

3. Let cookies stand on cookie sheets 1 minute. Remove cookies to wire racks; cool completely.

Makes about 3½ dozen cookies

Jumbo 3-Chip Cookies

Chocolate Almond Biscotti

1 package DUNCAN HINES® Moist Deluxe® Dark Chocolate Cake Mix
1 cup all-purpose flour
½ cup butter or margarine, melted
2 eggs
1 teaspoon almond extract
½ cup chopped almonds
    White chocolate, melted (optional)

1. Preheat oven to 350°F. Line 2 baking sheets with parchment paper.

2. Combine cake mix, flour, butter, eggs and almond extract in large bowl. Beat at low speed with electric mixer until well blended; stir in almonds. Divide dough in half. Shape each half into 12×2-inch log; place logs on prepared baking sheets. (Bake logs separately.)

3. Bake at 350°F for 30 to 35 minutes or until toothpick inserted in centers comes out clean. Remove logs from oven; cool on baking sheets 15 minutes. Using serrated knife, cut logs into ½-inch slices. Arrange slices on baking sheets. Bake biscotti 10 minutes. Remove to cooling racks; cool completely.

4. Dip one end of each biscotti in melted white chocolate, if desired. Allow white chocolate to set at room temperature before storing biscotti in airtight container. *Makes about 2½ dozen cookies*

Chocolate Macadamia Chippers

1 package (18 ounces) refrigerated chocolate chip cookie dough
3 tablespoons unsweetened cocoa powder
½ cup coarsely chopped macadamia nuts
    Powdered sugar (optional)

1. Preheat oven to 375°F. Remove dough from wrapper according to package directions.

2. Place dough in medium bowl; stir in cocoa until well blended. (Dough may be kneaded lightly, if desired.) Stir in nuts. Drop by heaping tablespoons 2 inches apart onto ungreased cookie sheets.

3. Bake 9 to 11 minutes or until almost set. Transfer to wire racks to cool completely. Dust lightly with powdered sugar, if desired.

Makes 2 dozen cookies

Chocolate Almond Biscotti

Baby Bottles

¾ **cup unsalted butter, softened**
¾ **cup sugar**
1 **egg**
1 **teaspoon vanilla**
1½ **cups cake flour**
1 **cup all-purpose flour**
¾ **teaspoon baking powder**
   White, pink and blue icings

1. Beat butter, sugar, egg and vanilla in large bowl at medium speed of electric mixer until creamy. Stir in flours and baking powder until well blended. Form dough into ball; wrap in plastic wrap and flatten. Refrigerate about 2 hours or until firm.

2. Preheat oven to 350°F. Lightly grease cookie sheets. Roll dough to ¼-inch thickness on floured surface. Cut out dough with 3½-inch baby bottle-shaped cookie cutter. Place cutouts 2 inches apart on ungreased baking sheets. Repeat with remaining dough and scraps.

3. Bake cutouts 8 to 10 minutes or until edges are golden. Cool on cookie sheets 1 to 2 minutes. Remove to wire racks to cool completely.

4. Decorate cookies with white, pink and blue icings as shown in photo or as desired. Let stand until icing is set.   *Makes 2 dozen cookies*

gift tip

These cute cookies are a fun way to celebrate a baby's arrival. They're also a great addition to a baby shower gift or a tasty baby shower favor. To make a party favor, wrap 2 cookies together in plastic wrap and tie with curling ribbon.

Baby Bottles

Chocolate Crackletops

2 cups all-purpose flour
2 teaspoons baking powder
2 cups granulated sugar
½ cup (1 stick) butter or margarine
4 squares (1 ounce each) unsweetened baking chocolate, chopped
4 eggs, lightly beaten
2 teaspoons vanilla extract
1¾ cups "M&M's"® Chocolate Mini Baking Bits
Additional granulated sugar

Combine flour and baking powder; set aside. In 2-quart saucepan over medium heat combine 2 cups sugar, butter and chocolate, stirring until butter and chocolate are melted; remove from heat. Gradually stir in eggs and vanilla. Stir in flour mixture until well blended. Chill mixture 1 hour. Stir in "M&M's"® Chocolate Mini Baking Bits; chill mixture an additional 1 hour.

Preheat oven to 350°F. Line cookie sheets with foil. With sugar-dusted hands, roll dough into 1-inch balls; roll balls in additional granulated sugar. Place about 2 inches apart onto prepared cookie sheets. Bake 10 to 12 minutes. *Do not overbake.* Cool completely on wire racks. Store in tightly covered container.

Makes about 5 dozen cookies

Coconut Macaroons

Prep Time: *10 minutes* • **Bake Time:** *15 to 17 minutes*

1 (14-ounce) can EAGLE® BRAND Sweetened Condensed Milk (NOT evaporated milk)
2 teaspoons vanilla extract
1 to 1½ teaspoons almond extract
2 (7-ounce) packages flaked coconut (5⅓ cups)

1. Preheat oven to 325°F. Line baking sheets with foil; grease and flour foil. Set aside.

2. In large mixing bowl, combine Eagle Brand, vanilla and almond extract. Stir in coconut. Drop by rounded teaspoonfuls onto prepared sheets; with spoon, slightly flatten each mound.

3. Bake 15 to 17 minutes or until golden. Remove from baking sheets; cool on wire racks. Store loosely covered at room temperature.

Makes about 4 dozen cookies

Chocolate Crackletops

Citrus-Ginger Cookies

1 Butter Flavor CRISCO® Stick or 1 cup Butter Flavor CRISCO®
   all-vegetable shortening
1½ cups granulated sugar
1 egg
2 tablespoons light corn syrup
1 teaspoon vanilla
3 cups all-purpose flour
3 teaspoons ground ginger
2 teaspoons baking soda
½ teaspoon fresh grated orange peel
½ teaspoon fresh grated lemon peel
½ teaspoon fresh grated lime peel

1. Combine shortening and sugar in large bowl. Beat at medium speed with electric mixer until well blended. Beat in egg, corn syrup and vanilla until well blended.

2. Combine flour, ginger and baking soda in small bowl. Add to creamed mixture. Add orange, lemon and lime peel until well blended.

3. Shape dough into two rolls about 2 inches in diameter. Wrap tightly in plastic wrap; refrigerate 3 hours or overnight.

4. Heat oven to 350°F.

5. Slice dough about ⅛ inch thick. Place 2 inches apart on ungreased cookie sheets. Bake at 350°F for 6 to 8 minutes or until lightly brown. Cool on cookie sheets 4 minutes; transfer to cooling racks. *Makes about 7 dozen cookies*

gift tip

For a delicious twist on a traditional hostess gift, decorate a metal tin with rubber stamp art and fill it with Citrus-Ginger Cookies and an assortment of uniquely flavored teas.

Mocha Mint Crisps

1 cup (2 sticks) butter or margarine, softened
1 cup sugar
1 egg
¼ cup light corn syrup
¼ teaspoon peppermint extract
1 teaspoon powdered instant coffee
1 teaspoon hot water
2 cups all-purpose flour
6 tablespoons HERSHEY¿S Cocoa
2 teaspoons baking soda
¼ teaspoon salt
    Mocha Mint Sugar (recipe follows)

1. Beat butter and sugar in large bowl until fluffy. Add egg, corn syrup and peppermint extract; beat until well blended. Dissolve instant coffee in hot water; stir into butter mixture.

2. Stir together flour, cocoa, baking soda and salt; gradually add to butter mixture, beating until well blended. Cover; refrigerate dough until firm enough to shape into balls.

3. Heat oven to 350°F.

4. Shape dough into 1-inch balls. Roll balls in Mocha Mint Sugar. Place on ungreased cookie sheet, about 2 inches apart.

5. Bake 8 to 10 minutes or until no imprint remains when touched lightly. Cool slightly; remove from cookie sheet to wire rack. Cool completely.

Makes about 4 dozen cookies

Mocha Mint Sugar: Stir together ¼ cup powdered sugar, 2 tablespoons finely crushed hard peppermint candies (about 6 candies) and 1½ teaspoons powdered instant coffee in small bowl.

Pecan Mini Kisses Cups

Prep Time: 25 minutes • *Chill Time:* 1 hour
Bake Time: 25 minutes • *Cool Time:* 1 hour

½ cup (1 stick) butter or margarine, softened
1 package (3 ounces) cream cheese, softened
1 cup all-purpose flour
1 egg
⅔ cup packed light brown sugar
1 tablespoon butter, melted
1 teaspoon vanilla extract
    Dash salt
72 HERSHEY'S MINI KISSES™ Milk Chocolates, divided
½ to ¾ cup coarsely chopped pecans

1. Beat ½ cup softened butter and cream cheese in medium bowl until blended. Add flour; beat well. Cover; refrigerate about 1 hour or until firm enough to handle.

2. Heat oven to 325°F. Stir together egg, brown sugar, 1 tablespoon melted butter, vanilla and salt in small bowl until well blended.

3. Shape chilled dough into 24 balls (1 inch each). Place balls in ungreased small muffin cups (1¾ inches in diameter). Press onto bottoms and up sides of cups. Place 2 Mini Kisses™ in each cup. Spoon about 1 teaspoon pecans over chocolate. Fill each cup with egg mixture.

4. Bake 25 minutes or until filling is set. Lightly press 1 Mini Kiss™ into center of each cookie. Cool in pan on wire rack.   *Makes 24 cups*

Tip: Use Mini Kisses™ Chocolates to decorate cakes, cupcakes, cookies and pies. Stir into slightly softened ice cream or sprinkle over top of a sundae for an added chocolate taste treat.

Pecan Mini Kisses Cups

Basic Icebox Cookie Dough

  1 **cup butter or margarine, softened**
  1 **cup sugar**
  1 **egg**
  1 **teaspoon vanilla**
2½ **cups all-purpose flour**
  1 **teaspoon baking powder**
 ½ **teaspoon salt**

Beat butter and sugar with an electric mixer. Add egg and vanilla; mix well. Combine flour, baking powder and salt. Gradually add to butter mixture; mix well. *Makes 4½ cups dough*

Maraschino Cherry Cookies: Add ½ cup chopped well-drained maraschino cherries to basic dough; divide dough in half. Form dough into 2 logs, 1½ inches in diameter. Wrap in waxed paper and refrigerate at least 6 hours. Cut into ¼-inch slices. Place 1 to 1½ inches apart on *ungreased* baking sheet. Bake in preheated 375°F oven 8 to 10 minutes. Remove to cooling rack. Repeat with remaining dough. Makes 6 to 7 dozen cookies.

Maraschino Date Pinwheels: Combine 8 ounces chopped pitted dates and ¼ cup water in small saucepan; bring to a boil. Reduce heat; simmer until thickened. Add ¾ cup chopped drained maraschino cherries; mix well and cool. Divide dough in half. Roll out each half to 12×10-inch rectangle on lightly floured surface. Spread half of cooled filling on each rectangle. Roll up beginning at long ends. Pinch ends of rolls to seal. Wrap in waxed paper and refrigerate at least 6 hours. Cut rolls into ¼-inch slices. Place 1 to 1½ inches apart on *ungreased* baking sheet. Bake in preheated 375°F oven about 10 to 14 minutes or until lightly browned. Remove to cooling rack. Makes 6 to 7 dozen cookies.

Maraschino Thumbprint Cookies: Shape dough into balls, using 2 teaspoons dough for each cookie. Press thumb in center of each ball. Place whole well-drained maraschino cherry in center of each depression. Brush with beaten egg white. For a nutty variation, before pressing with thumb and filling with cherry, roll each ball in beaten egg white, then in finely chopped pecans. Place 1 to 1½ inches apart on *ungreased* baking sheet. Bake in preheated 375°F oven 12 to 15 minutes. Remove to cooling rack. Makes 5 dozen cookies.

Favorite recipe from **Cherry Marketing Institute**

Left to right: Maraschino Date Pinwheels, Maraschino Thumbprint Cookies and Maraschino Cherry Cookies

Sugar Cookies

1 cup sugar
1 cup butter, softened
2 eggs
½ teaspoon *each* lemon extract and vanilla
3 cups all-purpose flour
1 teaspoon baking powder
¼ teaspoon salt
   Egg Yolk Paint (page 130)
   Liquid or paste food coloring
   Small, clean craft paintbrushes and clean kitchen sponges
   Royal Icing (page 130)
   Decorator Frosting (page 130)

1. Beat sugar and butter in large bowl until light and fluffy. Beat in eggs, lemon extract and vanilla until well blended (mixture will look grainy). Beat in 1 cup flour, baking powder and salt until well blended. Gradually add remaining 2 cups flour. Beat until soft dough forms. Divide dough into 3 discs; wrap in plastic wrap. Refrigerate 2 hours or until dough is firm.

2. Preheat oven to 375°F. Working with 1 disc at a time, unwrap dough and place on lightly floured surface. Roll out dough with lightly floured rolling pin to ⅛-inch thickness. Cut with floured 3- to 4-inch cookie cutters. Place cutouts 1 inch apart on *ungreased* cookie sheets. Press trimmings together and reroll.

3. To paint cookies before baking, prepare Egg Yolk Paint. Divide paint among several bowls; tint with liquid food coloring, if desired. Paint yolk paint onto unbaked cookies with small, clean craft paintbrushes. Bake 7 to 9 minutes or until cookies are set. Remove cookies to wire rack; cool completely.

4. To sponge paint cooled cookies, prepare Royal Icing. Divide icing among several bowls; tint with food coloring. For best results, use 2 to 3 shades of same color. (If icing is too thick, stir in water, 1 drop at a time, until of desired consistency.) Spread thin layer of icing on cookies to within ⅛ inch of edges. Let stand 30 minutes at room temperature or until icing is set.

5. Cut sponge into 1-inch squares. Dip sponge into tinted icing, scraping against side of bowl to remove excess icing. Press sponge on base icing several times until desired effect is achieved. Let stand 15 minutes or until icing is set.

6. To pipe additional decorations on cookies, prepare Decorator Frosting. Tint frosting as desired. Place each color frosting in piping bag fitted with small writing tip or resealable plastic freezer bags with one small corner cut off. Decorate as desired. Let stand until piping is set.   *Makes about 36 cookies*

continued on page 130

Sugar Cookies

Egg Yolk Paint: Combine 2 egg yolks and 2 teaspoons water in small bowl with fork until blended. Use to decorate unbaked cookies only. Makes about ⅓ cup.

Royal Icing

> **4 egg whites***
> **4 cups powdered sugar, sifted**
> **1 teaspoon almond extract or clear vanilla extract**** (optional)**

*Use only grade A clean, uncracked eggs.
**Icing remains very white when clear flavorings are used.

Beat egg whites in clean, large bowl with electric mixer at high speed until foamy. Gradually add sugar and almond extract, if desired. Beat until thickened.   *Makes 2 cups icing*

Note: When dry, Royal Icing is very hard and resistant to damage that can occur during shipping.

Decorator Frosting

> **¾ cup butter, softened**
> **4½ cups powdered sugar, sifted**
> **3 tablespoons water**
> **1 teaspoon vanilla**
> **¼ teaspoon lemon extract (optional)**

Beat butter in medium bowl until smooth. Add 2 cups sugar. Beat until light and fluffy. Add water, vanilla and lemon extract, if desired. Beat until well blended, scraping down side of bowl once. Beat in remaining 2½ cups sugar until mixture is creamy.   *Makes 2 cups frosting*

Note: This frosting is perfect for piping, but is less durable than Royal Icing. Bumping, stacking and handling may damage decorations.

Chocolate Chip Almond Biscotti

2¾ cups all-purpose flour
1½ teaspoons baking powder
¼ teaspoon salt
½ cup butter, softened
1 cup sugar
3 eggs
3 tablespoons almond-flavored liqueur
1 tablespoon water
1 cup mini semisweet chocolate chips
1 cup sliced almonds, toasted and chopped
   Melted milk chocolate (optional)

1. Place flour, baking powder and salt in medium bowl; stir to combine.

2. Beat butter and sugar in large bowl with electric mixer at medium speed until light and fluffy. Beat in eggs, one at a time. Beat in liqueur and water. Gradually add flour mixture. Beat at low speed just until blended. Stir in chips and almonds.

3. Divide dough into fourths. Spread each quarter evenly down center of waxed paper. Using waxed paper to hold dough, roll it back and forth to form 15-inch log. Wrap in plastic wrap. Refrigerate until firm, about 2 hours.

4. Preheat oven to 375°F. Lightly grease cookie sheet. Unwrap and place each log on prepared cookie sheet. With floured hands, shape each log 2 inches wide and ½ inch thick.

5. Bake 15 minutes. Remove cookie sheet from oven. Cut each log with serrated knife into 1-inch-thick diagonal slices. Place slices, cut side up, on cookie sheet; bake about 5 minutes. Turn cookies over; bake about 5 minutes or until cut surfaces are golden brown and cookies are dry. Remove cookies to wire racks; cool completely. Dip one end of each biscotti into melted milk chocolate, if desired; let stand on waxed paper until completely set. Store tightly covered at room temperature or freeze up to 3 months. (If chocolate-dipped cookies are frozen, chocolate may discolor.)

Makes about 4 dozen cookies

Milk Chocolate Florentine Cookies

⅔ cup butter
2 cups quick oats
1 cup granulated sugar
⅔ cup all-purpose flour
¼ cup light or dark corn syrup
¼ cup milk
1 teaspoon vanilla extract
¼ teaspoon salt
1¾ cups (11.5-ounce package) NESTLÉ® TOLL HOUSE® Milk Chocolate
   Morsels

PREHEAT oven to 375°F. Line baking sheets with foil.

MELT butter in medium saucepan; remove from heat. Stir in oats, sugar, flour, corn syrup, milk, vanilla extract and salt; mix well. Drop by level teaspoon, about 3 inches apart, onto prepared baking sheets. Spread thinly with rubber spatula.

BAKE for 6 to 8 minutes or until golden brown. Cool completely on baking sheets on wire racks. Peel foil from cookies.

MICROWAVE morsels in medium, microwave-safe bowl on MEDIUM-HIGH (70%) power for 1 minute; stir. Microwave at additional 10- to 20-second intervals, stirring until smooth. Spread thin layer of melted chocolate onto flat side of half the cookies. Top with remaining cookies.

Makes about 3½ dozen sandwich cookies

Milk Chocolate Florentine Cookies

Nutty Footballs

   1 **cup butter, softened**
   ½ **cup sugar**
   1 **egg**
   ½ **teaspoon vanilla**
   2 **cups all-purpose flour**
   ¼ **cup unsweetened cocoa powder**
   1 **cup finely chopped almonds**
      Colored icings (optional)
      White icing

1. Beat butter and sugar in large bowl until creamy. Add egg and vanilla; mix until well blended. Stir together flour and cocoa; gradually add to butter mixture, beating until well blended. Add almonds; beat until well blended. Shape dough into disc. Wrap dough in plastic wrap and refrigerate 30 minutes.

2. Preheat oven to 350°F. Lightly grease cookie sheets. Roll out dough on floured surface to ¼-inch thickness. Cut dough with 2½- to 3-inch football-shaped cookie cutter.* Place 2 inches apart on prepared cookie sheets.

3. Bake 10 to 12 minutes or until set. Cool on cookie sheets 1 to 2 minutes. Remove to wire racks; cool completely. Decorate with colored icings, if desired. Pipe white icing onto footballs to make laces.   *Makes 2 dozen cookies*

*If you do not have a football-shaped cookie cutter, shape 3 tablespoonfuls dough into ovals. Place 3 inches apart on prepared cookie sheets. Flatten ovals to ¼-inch thickness; taper ends. Bake as directed.

gift tip

These cookies are a great gift for the football fan in your life. Decorate them in the colors of his or her favorite team and arrange them on a plate lined with green napkins. You're sure to score extra points!

Nutty Footballs

Lollipop Cookies

3 cups all-purpose flour
1 teaspoon baking powder
1⅓ cups granulated sugar
1 cup butter, softened
2 eggs
2 teaspoons vanilla
2 ounces unsweetened chocolate, melted
Craft sticks (available where cake decorating supplies are sold)
Royal Icing (page 130)
Liquid or paste food colors
Decorator Frosting (page 130)

1. Preheat oven to 350°F. Mix flour and baking powder in bowl. Beat sugar and butter in large bowl until light and fluffy, scraping bowl once. Beat in eggs and vanilla until blended. Add flour mixture. Beat until blended, scraping bowl once.

2. Remove half of dough from bowl; form into disc. Wrap disc in plastic wrap; refrigerate while working with remaining dough. Add melted chocolate to remaining dough in bowl. Beat until well blended.

3. Place chocolate dough on lightly floured surface; press into 6-inch square. Cut evenly into 16 squares; roll each into a ball. Place balls 3 inches apart on ungreased baking sheets. Place craft stick under each ball. Flatten balls into 2½-inch circles. Bake 10 to 12 minutes or until edges are set. Immediately remove cookies to wire racks; cool. Repeat with remaining vanilla dough.

4. Prepare Royal Icing. Divide icing among bowls; tint with desired food colors. (If using paste colors, stir in water 1 drop at a time, until thin enough to drizzle.) Place large sheet of foil on counter. Place cookies on foil. Spread thin layer of icing on cookies to within ⅛ inch of edge. Dip spoon into contrasting color of icing. Drizzle or drop icing onto base color. Swirl colors with toothpick. Stand 30 minutes or until set.

5. To add additional piped decorations, stir additional sifted powdered sugar into Royal Icing until thick enough to hold shape when dropped from spoon. Spoon icing into resealable plastic freezer bag; cut off one tiny corner of bag. Pipe icing onto cookies as desired. Stand 1 hour or until set.

6. To assemble lollipops, prepare Decorator Frosting, omitting lemon extract. Spread 1½ tablespoons frosting on flat side of chocolate cookie to within ¼ inch of edge. Place vanilla cookie, flat-side down, on frosting. Press cookies together. Repeat. Stand 20 minutes or until set. Store tightly covered at room temperature for up to 2 weeks. *Makes 16 lollipops*

Lollipop Cookies

Greeting Card Cookies

½ cup (1 stick) butter or margarine, softened
¾ cup sugar
1 egg
1 teaspoon vanilla extract
1½ cups all-purpose flour
⅓ cup HERSHEY'S Cocoa
½ teaspoon baking powder
½ teaspoon baking soda
¼ teaspoon salt
Decorative Frosting (recipe follows)

1. Beat butter, sugar, egg and vanilla in large bowl until fluffy. Stir together flour, cocoa, baking powder, baking soda and salt; add to butter mixture, blending well. Refrigerate about 1 hour or until firm enough to roll. Cut cardboard rectangle for pattern, 2½×4 inches; wrap in plastic wrap.

2. Heat oven to 350°F. Lightly grease cookie sheet. On lightly floured board or between two pieces of wax paper, roll out half of dough to ¼-inch thickness. For each cookie, place pattern on dough; cut through dough around pattern with sharp paring knife. (Save dough trimmings and reroll for remaining cookies.) Carefully place cutouts on prepared cookie sheet.

3. Bake 8 to 10 minutes or until set. Cool 1 minute on cookie sheet. (If cookies have lost their shape, trim irregular edges while cookies are still hot.) Carefully transfer to wire rack. Repeat procedure with remaining dough.

4. Prepare Decorative Frosting; spoon into pastry bag fitted with decorating tip. Pipe names or greetings onto cookies; decorate as desired.

Makes about 12 cookies

Decorative Frosting

3 cups powdered sugar
⅓ cup shortening
2 to 3 tablespoons milk
Food color (optional)

Beat sugar and shortening in small bowl; gradually add milk, beating until smooth and slightly thickened. Cover until ready to use. If desired, divide frosting into two bowls; tint each a different color with food color.

Cheers

Best
Wishes

Happy
Birthday

Greeting Card Cookies

Canned Peanut Butter Candy Cookies

¾ cup chunky peanut butter
½ cup butter, softened
 1 cup packed light brown sugar
½ teaspoon baking powder
½ teaspoon baking soda
 1 egg
1½ teaspoons vanilla
1¼ cups all-purpose flour
 2 cups quartered miniature peanut butter cups
⅓ cup milk chocolate chips or chopped milk chocolate bar

1. Beat peanut butter and butter in large bowl of electric mixer at medium speed until well blended. Beat in brown sugar, baking powder and baking soda until blended. Beat in egg and vanilla until well blended. Beat in flour at low speed just until mixed. Stir in peanut butter cups. Cover and refrigerate 1 hour or until firm.

2. Preheat oven to 375°F. For test cookie, measure inside diameter of container. Form ⅓ cup dough into ¼-inch-thick disc, about 2 inches in diameter less than the diameter of container. (One-third cup dough patted into 4-inch disc yields 5-inch cookie. Measure amount of dough used and diameter of cookie before and after baking. Make adjustments before making remaining cookies.)

3. Place dough on *ungreased* cookie sheets. Bake 10 minutes or until lightly browned. Remove to wire racks; cool completely.

4. Place chocolate chips in small resealable plastic food storage bag; seal bag. Microwave at MEDIUM (50% power) 1 minute. Turn bag over; microwave at MEDIUM 1 minute or until melted. Knead bag until chocolate is smooth. Cut off very tiny corner of bag; pipe chocolate decoratively onto cookies. Let stand until chocolate is set.

5. Stack cookies between layers of waxed paper in container. Store loosely covered at room temperature up to 1 week. *Makes 9 (5-inch) cookies*

Canned Peanut Butter Candy Cookies

Anna's Icing Oatmeal Sandwich Cookies

Cookies
- ¾ Butter Flavor CRISCO® Stick or ¾ cup Butter Flavor CRISCO® all-vegetable shortening plus additional for greasing
- 1¼ cups firmly packed light brown sugar
- 1 egg
- ⅓ cup milk
- 1½ teaspoons vanilla
- 3 cups quick oats, uncooked
- 1 cup all-purpose flour
- ½ teaspoon baking soda
- ½ teaspoon salt

Frosting
- 2 cups confectioners' sugar
- ¼ Butter Flavor CRISCO® Stick or ¼ cup Butter Flavor CRISCO® all-vegetable shortening
- ½ teaspoon vanilla
- Milk

1. Heat oven to 350°F. Grease baking sheets with shortening. Place sheets of foil on countertop for cooling cookies.

2. For cookies, combine ¾ cup shortening, brown sugar, egg, milk and vanilla in large bowl. Beat at medium speed of electric mixer until well blended.

3. Combine oats, flour, baking soda and salt. Mix into creamed mixture at low speed just until blended.

4. Drop rounded measuring tablespoonfuls of dough 2 inches apart onto prepared baking sheets.

5. Bake one sheet at a time at 375°F for 10 to 12 minutes, or until lightly browned. *Do not overbake.* Cool 2 minutes on baking sheet. Remove cookies to foil to cool completely.

6. For frosting, combine confectioners' sugar, shortening and vanilla in medium bowl. Beat at low speed, adding enough milk for good spreading consistency. Spread on bottoms of half the cookies. Top with remaining cookies.

Makes about 16 sandwich cookies

Anna's Icing Oatmeal Sandwich Cookies

Double Lemon Delights

2¼ cups all-purpose flour
½ teaspoon baking powder
½ teaspoon salt
1 cup butter, softened
¾ cup granulated sugar
1 egg
2 tablespoons grated lemon peel, divided
1 teaspoon vanilla
   Additional sugar
1 cup powdered sugar
4 to 5 teaspoons lemon juice

1. Preheat oven to 375°F.

2. Combine flour, baking powder and salt in small bowl; set aside. Beat butter and granulated sugar in large bowl of electric mixer at medium speed until light and fluffy. Beat in egg, 1 tablespoon lemon peel and vanilla until well blended. Gradually beat in flour mixture on low speed until blended.

3. Drop dough by level ¼ cupfuls onto *ungreased* cookie sheets, spacing 3 inches apart. Flatten dough until 3 inches in diameter with bottom of glass that has been dipped in additional sugar.

4. Bake 12 to 14 minutes or until cookies are just set and edges are golden brown. Cool on cookie sheets 2 minutes; transfer to wire racks. Cool completely.

5. Combine powdered sugar, lemon juice and remaining 1 tablespoon lemon peel in small bowl; drizzle mixture over cookies. Let stand until icing is set.

Makes about 1 dozen (4-inch) cookies

Variation: To make smaller cookies, drop 2 tablespoons dough 2 inches apart on *ungreased* cookie sheets. Bake 8 to 10 minutes or until cookies are just set and edges are golden brown. Cool on cookie sheets 2 minutes; transfer to wire racks. Cool completely. Continue with Step 5. Makes about 2 dozen cookies.

Double Lemon Delights

Double-Dipped Hazelnut Crisps

¾ cup semisweet chocolate chips
1¼ cups all-purpose flour
¾ cup powdered sugar
⅔ cup whole hazelnuts, toasted, hulled and finely ground*
¼ teaspoon instant espresso powder
   Dash salt
½ cup butter, softened
2 teaspoons vanilla
4 squares (1 ounce each) bittersweet or semisweet chocolate
2 teaspoons shortening, divided
4 ounces white chocolate

To grind hazelnuts, place in food processor or blender. Process until thoroughly ground with a dry, not pasty, texture.

1. Preheat oven to 350°F. Lightly grease cookie sheets or line with parchment paper. Melt chocolate chips in top of double boiler over hot, not boiling, water. Remove from heat; cool. Blend flour, powdered sugar, hazelnuts, espresso powder and salt in large bowl. Blend in butter, melted chocolate and vanilla until dough is stiff but smooth. (If dough is too soft to handle, cover and refrigerate until firm.)

2. Roll out dough, ¼ at a time, to ⅛-inch thickness on lightly floured surface. Cut out with 2-inch scalloped round cutters. Place 2 inches apart on prepared cookie sheets. Bake 8 minutes or until not quite firm. (Cookies should not brown. They will puff up during baking, then flatten again.) Remove to wire racks to cool.

3. Place bittersweet chocolate and 1 teaspoon shortening in small bowl. Place bowl over hot water; stir until chocolate is melted and smooth. Dip cookies, 1 at a time, halfway into bittersweet chocolate. Place on waxed paper; refrigerate until chocolate is set. Repeat melting process with white chocolate. Dip plain halves of cookies into white chocolate; refrigerate until set. Store cookies in airtight container in cool place. (If cookies are frozen, chocolate may discolor.)

Makes about 4 dozen cookies

Orange Pecan Refrigerator Cookies

2⅓ cups all-purpose flour
½ teaspoon baking soda
¼ teaspoon salt
½ cup butter or margarine, softened
½ cup packed brown sugar
½ cup granulated sugar
1 egg, lightly beaten
Grated peel of 1 SUNKIST® orange
3 tablespoons fresh squeezed SUNKIST® orange juice
¾ cup pecan pieces

In bowl, stir together flour, baking soda and salt. In large bowl, blend together butter, brown sugar and granulated sugar. Add egg, orange peel and juice; beat well. Stir in pecans. Gradually beat in flour mixture. (Dough will be stiff.) Divide mixture in half and shape each half (on long piece of waxed paper) into roll about 1¼ inches in diameter and 12 inches long. Roll up tightly in waxed paper. Chill several hours or overnight.

Cut into ¼-inch slices and arrange on lightly greased cookie sheets. Bake at 350°F for 10 to 12 minutes or until lightly browned. Cool on wire racks.

Makes about 6 dozen cookies

Chocolate Filled Sandwich Cookies: Cut each roll into ⅛-inch slices and bake as above. When cool, to make each sandwich cookie, spread about 1 teaspoon canned chocolate fudge frosting on bottom side of 1 cookie; cover with second cookie of same shape. Makes about 4 dozen sandwich cookies.

gift tip

For a special touch, dip half of each cookie in melted white chocolate, or drizzle the cookies with a glaze of 1¼ cups powdered sugar and 2 tablespoons orange juice. Then sprinkle with chopped pecans.

Brownies & Bars

Chocolate Espresso Brownies

4 squares (1 ounce each) unsweetened chocolate
1 cup sugar
¼ cup Dried Plum Purée (recipe follows) or prepared dried plum butter
3 egg whites
1 to 2 tablespoons instant espresso coffee powder
1 teaspoon baking powder
1 teaspoon salt
1 teaspoon vanilla
½ cup all-purpose flour
　 Powdered sugar (optional)

Preheat oven to 350°F. Coat 8-inch square baking pan with vegetable cooking spray. In small heavy saucepan, melt chocolate over very low heat, stirring until melted and smooth. Remove from heat; cool. In mixer bowl, beat chocolate and remaining ingredients except flour and powdered sugar at medium speed until well blended; mix in flour. Spread batter evenly in prepared pan. Bake in center of oven about 30 minutes until pick inserted into center comes out clean. Cool completely in pan on wire rack. Dust with powdered sugar. Cut into 1⅓-inch squares.   *Makes 36 brownies*

Dried Plum Purée: Combine 1⅓ cups (8 ounces) pitted dried plums and 6 tablespoons hot water in container of food processor or blender. Pulse on and off until dried plums are finely chopped and smooth. Store leftovers in a covered container in the refrigerator for up to two months. Makes 1 cup.

Favorite recipe from **California Dried Plum Board**

Chocolate Espresso Brownies

Chocolate Nut Bars

Prep Time: 10 minutes • Bake Time: 33 to 38 minutes

1¾ **cups graham cracker crumbs**
½ **cup (1 stick) butter or margarine, melted**
1 **(14-ounce) can EAGLE® BRAND Sweetened Condensed Milk (NOT**
    evaporated milk)
2 **cups (12 ounces) semi-sweet chocolate chips, divided**
1 **teaspoon vanilla extract**
1 **cup chopped nuts**

1. Preheat oven to 375°F. In medium mixing bowl, combine crumbs and butter; press firmly on bottom of ungreased 13×9-inch baking pan. Bake 8 minutes. Reduce oven temperature to 350°F.

2. In small saucepan, melt Eagle Brand with 1 cup chips and vanilla. Spread chocolate mixture over prepared crust. Top with remaining 1 cup chips and nuts; press down firmly.

3. Bake 25 to 30 minutes. Cool. Chill, if desired. Cut into bars. Store loosely covered at room temperature. *Makes 24 to 36 bars*

Macaroon Brownies

1 **(21-ounce) package DUNCAN HINES® Family-Style Chewy Fudge**
    Brownie Mix
2 **egg whites**
½ **cup granulated sugar**
¼ **teaspoon almond extract**
1 **cup finely chopped almonds**
1 **cup flaked coconut**

1. Preheat oven to 350°F. Grease bottom only of 13×9-inch pan.

2. Prepare brownies as directed on package for cake-like brownies. Bake at 350°F for 25 minutes or until set. Place egg whites in medium mixing bowl. Beat at high speed with electric mixer until foamy and double in volume. Beat in sugar gradually, beating until meringue forms firm peaks. Add almond extract. Fold in almonds and coconut. Spread over warm brownies. Bake at 350°F for 12 to 14 minutes or until meringue is set and lightly browned. Cool completely in pan. Cut into bars. *Makes 24 brownies*

Note: Spread the meringue to the edges of the pan to prevent meringue from shrinking.

Chocolate Nut Bars

Double Mint Brownies

  1 (21-ounce) package DUNCAN HINES® Family-Style Chewy Recipe
      Fudge Brownie Mix
  1 egg
  ⅓ cup water
  ⅓ cup vegetable oil plus additional for greasing
  ½ teaspoon peppermint extract
 24 chocolate-covered peppermint patties (1½ inches each)
  1 cup confectioners' sugar, divided
  4 teaspoons milk, divided
    Red food coloring
    Green food coloring

1. Preheat oven to 350°F. Grease bottom only of 13×9×2-inch pan. Combine brownie mix, egg, water, oil and peppermint extract in large bowl. Stir with spoon until well blended, about 50 strokes. Spread in prepared pan. Bake brownies following package directions. Place peppermint patties on warm brownies. Cool completely.

2. Combine ½ cup confectioners' sugar, 2 teaspoons milk and 1 drop red food coloring in small bowl. Stir until smooth. Place in small resealable plastic bag; set aside. Repeat with remaining ½ cup confectioners' sugar, remaining 2 teaspoons milk and 1 drop green food coloring. Cut pinpoint hole in bottom corner of each bag. Drizzle pink and green glazes over brownies as shown. Allow glazes to set before cutting into bars. *Makes 24 brownies*

Tip: To prevent overdone edges and underdone center, wrap foil strips around outside edges of pan (do not cover bottom or top). Bake as directed above.

Double Mint Brownies

Mini Kisses Coconut Macaroon Bars

Prep Time: *15 minutes •* ***Bake Time:*** *35 minutes •* ***Cool Time:*** *9 hours*

3¾ **cups (10-ounce package) MOUNDS® Sweetened Coconut Flakes**
¾ **cup sugar**
¼ **cup all-purpose flour**
¼ **teaspoon salt**
3 **egg whites**
1 **whole egg, slightly beaten**
1 **teaspoon almond extract**
1 **cup HERSHEY'S MINI KISSES™ Milk Chocolates**

1. Heat oven to 350°F. Lightly grease 9-inch square baking pan.

2. Stir together coconut, sugar, flour and salt in large bowl. Add egg whites, whole egg and almond extract; stir until well blended. Stir in Mini Kisses™. Spread mixture into prepared pan, covering all chocolate pieces with coconut mixture.

3. Bake 35 minutes or until lightly browned. Cool completely in pan on wire rack. Cover with foil; allow to stand at room temperature about 8 hours or overnight. Cut into bars.   *Makes about 24 bars*

Variation: Omit Mini Kisses™ in batter. Immediately after removing pan from oven, place desired number of chocolate pieces on top, pressing down lightly. Cool completely. Cut into bars.

gift tip

For a more fancy appearance, try cutting these delicious bars into diamonds. First, cut straight lines 1 or 1½ inches apart the length of the baking pan, then cut straight lines 1½ inches apart diagonally across the pan.

Mini Kisses Coconut Macaroon Bars

Fudge Topped Brownies

1 cup (2 sticks) butter or margarine, melted
2 cups sugar
1 cup all-purpose flour
⅔ cup unsweetened cocoa
½ teaspoon baking powder
2 eggs
½ cup milk
3 teaspoons vanilla extract, divided
1 cup chopped nuts, if desired
2 cups (12 ounces) semi-sweet chocolate chips
1 (14-ounce) can EAGLE® BRAND Sweetened Condensed Milk (NOT evaporated milk)
Dash salt

1. Preheat oven to 350°F. In large mixing bowl, combine butter, sugar, flour, cocoa, baking powder, eggs, milk and 1½ teaspoons vanilla; mix well. Stir in nuts, if desired. Spread in greased 13×9-inch baking pan. Bake 40 minutes or until brownies begin to pull away from sides of pan.

2. Meanwhile, in heavy saucepan over low heat, melt chips with Eagle Brand, remaining 1½ teaspoons vanilla and salt. Remove from heat. Immediately spread over hot brownies. Cool. Chill. Cut into bars. Store covered at room temperature.

Makes 3 to 3½ dozen brownies

*Fudge Topped
Brownies*

Cookie Pizza

Prep Time: 15 minutes • **Bake Time:** 14 minutes

1 (18-ounce) package refrigerated sugar cookie dough
2 cups (12 ounces) semi-sweet chocolate chips
1 (14-ounce) can EAGLE® BRAND Sweetened Condensed Milk (NOT evaporated milk)
2 cups candy-coated milk chocolate candies
2 cups miniature marshmallows
½ cup peanuts

1. Preheat oven 375°F. Press cookie dough into 2 ungreased 12-inch pizza pans. Bake 10 minutes or until golden. Remove from oven.

2. In medium-sized saucepan, melt chips with Eagle Brand. Spread over crusts. Sprinkle with milk chocolate candies, marshmallows and peanuts.

3. Bake 4 minutes or until marshmallows are lightly toasted. Cool. Cut into wedges.   *Makes 2 pizzas (24 servings)*

White Chocolate Cranberry Cookie Bars

2 cups all-purpose flour
1 teaspoon baking powder
1 teaspoon salt
4 eggs
1¾ cups sugar
1 teaspoon vanilla extract
1 bag (12 ounces) white chocolate chips (2 cups), divided
½ cup (1 stick) IMPERIAL® Spread
1 cup dried cranberries

Preheat oven to 350°F. Grease 13×9-inch baking pan; set aside.

In medium bowl, combine flour, baking powder and salt; set aside. In small bowl, with wire whisk, beat eggs, sugar and vanilla; set aside.

In medium saucepan, melt 1 cup white chocolate chips with spread over low heat, stirring occasionally. Remove from heat; let cool slightly. While stirring chocolate mixture, slowly stir in egg mixture, then flour mixture until blended. Stir in remaining 1 cup chips and cranberries. Evenly pour into prepared pan.

Bake uncovered 40 minutes or until center springs back when lightly touched. On wire rack, cool completely. To serve, cut into bars.   *Makes 2 dozen bars*

Cookie Pizza

Pecan Pie Bars

¾ **cup butter**
½ **cup powdered sugar**
1½ **cups all-purpose flour**
3 **eggs**
2 **cups coarsely chopped pecans**
1 **cup granulated sugar**
1 **cup light corn syrup**
2 **tablespoons butter, melted**
1 **teaspoon vanilla**

1. Preheat oven to 350°F. For crust, beat ¾ cup butter in large bowl with electric mixer at medium speed until smooth. Add powdered sugar; beat at medium speed until well blended. Add flour gradually, beating at low speed after each addition. (Mixture will be crumbly but presses together easily.)

2. Press dough evenly into *ungreased* 13×9-inch baking pan. Press mixture slightly up sides of pan (less than ¼ inch) to form lip to hold filling. Bake 20 to 25 minutes or until golden brown.

3. Meanwhile, for filling, beat eggs lightly in medium bowl with fork. Add pecans, granulated sugar, corn syrup, 2 tablespoons melted butter and vanilla; mix well. Pour filling over partially baked crust. Return to oven; bake 35 to 40 minutes or until filling is set.

4. Loosen edges with knife. Let cool completely on wire rack before cutting into squares. Cover and refrigerate until 10 to 15 minutes before serving time. *Do not freeze.*   *Makes about 4 dozen bars*

gift tip | *For an easy, festive garnish for these classic bars, drizzle them with melted chocolate. Or, dip a pecan half into melted chocolate and place in the center of each bar.*

SUGAR

FL[U]

Pecan Pie Bars

Pecan Caramel Brownies

50 candy caramels, unwrapped
2 tablespoons milk
1½ cups granulated sugar
1 cup all-purpose flour
1 cup butter, melted
4 eggs
⅔ cup unsweetened cocoa powder
2 teaspoons vanilla
½ teaspoon baking powder
¼ teaspoon salt
1 cup (6 ounces) semisweet chocolate chips
⅓ cup pecan halves
Cocoa Glaze (recipe follows)

Preheat oven to 350°F. Butter 13×9-inch pan. Melt caramels with milk in small heavy saucepan over low heat, stirring until caramels melt completely. Keep warm. Combine granulated sugar, flour, butter, eggs, cocoa, vanilla, baking powder and salt in large bowl. Beat with mixer at medium speed until smooth. Spread half of batter in prepared pan. Bake 15 minutes. Remove from oven; sprinkle with chocolate chips. Drizzle melted caramel mixture over top, covering evenly. Spoon remaining batter over all. Return to oven; bake 20 minutes. Do not overbake. Meanwhile, toast pecan halves in another pan in same oven 3 to 5 minutes. Prepare Cocoa Glaze. Pour over warm brownies; arrange toasted pecans on top. Cool completely in pan on wire rack. Cut into 2-inch squares.   *Makes about 2 dozen brownies*

Cocoa Glaze

2 tablespoons butter or margarine
2 tablespoons unsweetened cocoa powder
2 tablespoons milk
Dash salt
1 cup powdered sugar
1 teaspoon vanilla

Combine butter, cocoa, milk and salt in small heavy saucepan. Bring to a boil over medium heat, stirring constantly. Remove from heat; add powdered sugar and beat until smooth. Stir in vanilla.

Coconutty "M&M's"® Brownies

    6 squares (1 ounce each) semi-sweet chocolate
    ¾ cup granulated sugar
    ½ cup (1 stick) butter
    2 eggs
    1 tablespoon vegetable oil
    1 teaspoon vanilla extract
  1¼ cups all-purpose flour
    3 tablespoons unsweetened cocoa powder
    1 teaspoon baking powder
    ½ teaspoon salt
  1½ cups "M&M's"® Chocolate Mini Baking Bits, divided
       Coconut Topping (recipe follows)

Preheat oven to 350°F. Lightly grease 8×8×2-inch baking pan; set aside. In small saucepan combine chocolate, sugar and butter over low heat; stir constantly until chocolate is melted. Remove from heat; let cool slightly. In large bowl beat eggs, oil and vanilla; stir in chocolate mixture until well blended. In medium bowl combine flour, cocoa powder, baking powder and salt; add to chocolate mixture. Stir in 1 cup "M&M's"® Chocolate Mini Baking Bits. Spread batter evenly in prepared pan. Bake 35 to 40 minutes or until toothpick inserted in center comes out clean. Cool completely on wire rack. Prepare Coconut Topping. Spread over brownies; sprinkle with remaining ½ cup "M&M's"® Chocolate Mini Baking Bits. Cut into bars. Store in tightly covered container.   *Makes 16 brownies*

Coconut Topping

    ½ cup (1 stick) butter
    ⅓ cup firmly packed light brown sugar
    ⅓ cup light corn syrup
    1 cup sweetened shredded coconut, toasted*
    ¾ cup chopped pecans
    1 teaspoon vanilla extract

To toast coconut, spread evenly on cookie sheet. Toast in preheated 350°F oven 7 to 8 minutes or until golden brown, stirring occasionally.

In large saucepan melt butter over medium heat; add brown sugar and corn syrup, stirring constantly until thick and bubbly. Remove from heat and stir in remaining ingredients.

Chocolate Chip Candy Cookie Bars

1⅔ cups all-purpose flour
2 tablespoons plus 1½ cups sugar, divided
¾ teaspoon baking powder
1 cup (2 sticks) cold butter or margarine, divided
1 egg, slightly beaten
½ cup plus 2 tablespoons (5-ounce can) evaporated milk, divided
2 cups (12-ounce package) HERSHEY'S Semi-Sweet Chocolate Chips, divided
½ cup light corn syrup
1½ cups sliced almonds

1. Heat oven to 375°F.

2. Stir together flour, 2 tablespoons sugar and baking powder in medium bowl; using pastry blender, cut in ½ cup butter until mixture forms coarse crumbs. Stir in egg and 2 tablespoons evaporated milk; stir until mixture holds together in ball shape. Press onto bottom and ¼ inch up sides of 15½×10½×1-inch jelly-roll pan.

3. Bake 8 to 10 minutes or until lightly browned; remove from oven, leaving oven on. Sprinkle 1½ cups chocolate chips evenly over crust; do not disturb chips.

4. Place remaining 1½ cups sugar, remaining ½ cup butter, remaining ½ cup evaporated milk and corn syrup in 3-quart saucepan. Cook over medium heat, stirring constantly, until mixture boils; stir in almonds. Continue cooking and stirring to 240°F on candy thermometer (soft-ball stage) or until small amount of mixture, when dropped into very cold water, forms a soft ball which flattens when removed from water. (Bulb of candy thermometer should not rest on bottom of saucepan.) Remove from heat. Immediately spoon almond mixture evenly over chips and crust; do not spread.

5. Bake 10 to 15 minutes or just until almond mixture is golden brown. Remove from oven; cool 5 minutes. Sprinkle remaining ½ cup chips over top; cool completely. Cut into bars.   *Makes about 48 bars*

Chocolate Chip Candy Cookie Bars

Lemon Bars

Crust
- 2 cups all-purpose flour
- ½ cup powdered sugar
- 1 cup (2 sticks) butter or margarine, softened

Filling
- 1 can (14 ounces) NESTLÉ® CARNATION® Sweetened Condensed Milk
- 4 eggs
- ⅔ cup lemon juice
- 1 tablespoon all-purpose flour
- 1 teaspoon baking powder
- ¼ teaspoon salt
- 4 drops yellow food coloring (optional)
- 1 tablespoon grated lemon peel
- Sifted powdered sugar (optional)

PREHEAT oven to 350°F.

For Crust

COMBINE flour and sugar in medium bowl. Cut in butter with pastry blender or two knives until mixture is crumbly. Press lightly onto bottom and halfway up sides of ungreased 13×9-inch baking pan.

BAKE for 20 minutes.

For Filling

BEAT sweetened condensed milk and eggs in large mixer bowl until fluffy. Beat in lemon juice, flour, baking powder, salt and food coloring just until blended. Fold in lemon peel; pour over crust.

BAKE for 20 to 25 minutes or until filling is set and crust is golden brown. Cool in pan on wire rack. Refrigerate for about 2 hours. Cut into bars; sprinkle with powdered sugar.   *Makes 4 dozen bars*

Lemon Bars

Easy Double Chocolate Chip Brownies

2 cups (12-ounce package) NESTLÉ® TOLL HOUSE® Semi-Sweet
   Chocolate Morsels, *divided*
½ cup (1 stick) butter or margarine, cut into pieces
3 eggs
1¼ cups all-purpose flour
1 cup granulated sugar
1 teaspoon vanilla extract
¼ teaspoon baking soda
½ cup chopped nuts

PREHEAT oven to 350°F. Grease 13×9-inch baking pan.

MELT *1 cup* morsels and butter in large, *heavy-duty* saucepan over low heat;
stir until smooth. Remove from heat. Stir in eggs. Stir in flour, sugar, vanilla
extract and baking soda. Stir in *remaining* morsels and nuts. Spread into
prepared baking pan.

BAKE for 18 to 22 minutes or until wooden pick inserted in center comes out
slightly sticky. Cool completely in pan on wire rack.

Makes 2 dozen brownies

White Chip Island Blondies

1 cup plus 2 tablespoons all-purpose flour
1 teaspoon baking powder
¼ teaspoon salt
¾ cup packed light brown sugar
⅓ cup butter or margarine, softened
½ teaspoon vanilla extract
1 egg
1 cup (6 ounces) NESTLÉ® TOLL HOUSE® Premier White Morsels
½ cup coarsely chopped macadamia nuts
½ cup toasted coconut

PREHEAT oven to 350°F. Grease 9-inch-square baking pan.

COMBINE flour, baking powder and salt in medium bowl. Beat sugar, butter and
vanilla extract in large mixer bowl until creamy. Beat in egg. Gradually beat in
flour mixture. Stir in morsels, nuts and coconut. Press into prepared baking pan.

BAKE for 20 to 25 minutes or until golden brown. Cool completely in pan on
wire rack. Cut into bars.

Makes about 16 bars

Easy Double Chocolate Chip Brownies

Chocolate Coconut Bars

COOKIE BASE
- ⅔ cup sugar
- ½ Butter Flavor CRISCO® Stick or ½ cup Butter Flavor CRISCO® all-vegetable shortening plus additional for greasing
- ¼ cup cocoa
- 1 egg
- 1 tablespoon water
- 1¼ cups all-purpose flour
- ¼ teaspoon salt

FILLING
- 1 can (14 ounces) sweetened condensed milk (not evaporated milk)
- 3 tablespoons all-purpose flour
- 1 teaspoon vanilla
- ¾ cup semisweet chocolate chips
- ⅔ cup chopped walnuts
- ½ cup flake coconut

1. Heat oven to 350°F. Grease 13×9×2-inch pan with shortening. Place cooling rack on countertop.

2. For cookie base, combine sugar, shortening, cocoa, egg and water in large bowl. Beat at medium speed of electric mixer until well blended.

3. Combine 1¼ cups flour and salt. Add gradually to creamed mixture at low speed. Beat just until blended. Press into bottom of greased pan.

4. Bake at 350°F for 10 minutes. *Do not overbake.*

5. For filling, combine condensed milk, 3 tablespoons flour and vanilla. Stir with spoon until well blended. Stir in chocolate chips, nuts and coconut. Spoon over baked cookie base. Spread carefully to cover.

6. Return to oven. Bake for 20 minutes. *Do not overbake.* Remove pan to cooling rack. Cut into bars about 1½×1½ inches.

Makes about 4 dozen bars

Chocolate Coconut Bars

Marbled Cherry Brownies

Prep Time: 25 minutes • Bake Time: 35 minutes • Cool Time: 1½ hours

Cherry Cream Filling (recipe follows)
½ **cup (1 stick) butter or margarine, melted**
⅓ **cup HERSHEY'S Cocoa**
2 **eggs**
1 **cup sugar**
1 **teaspoon vanilla extract**
½ **cup all-purpose flour**
½ **teaspoon baking powder**
¼ **teaspoon salt**

1. Prepare Cherry Cream Filling; set aside. Heat oven to 350°F. Grease 9-inch square baking pan.

2. Stir butter and cocoa in small bowl until well blended. Beat eggs in medium bowl until foamy. Gradually add sugar and vanilla, beating until well blended. Stir together flour, baking powder and salt; add to egg mixture. Add cocoa mixture; stir until well blended.

3. Spread half of chocolate batter into prepared pan; cover with cherry filling. Drop spoonfuls of remaining chocolate batter over filling. With knife or spatula, gently swirl chocolate batter into filling for marbled effect.

4. Bake 35 to 40 minutes or until brownies begin to pull away from sides of pan. Cool; cut into squares. Cover; refrigerate leftover brownies. Bring to room temperature to serve.   *Makes about 16 brownies*

Cherry Cream Filling

1 **package (3 ounces) cream cheese, softened**
¼ **cup sugar**
1 **egg**
½ **teaspoon vanilla extract**
¼ **teaspoon almond extract**
⅓ **cup chopped maraschino cherries, well drained**
1 **to 2 drops red food color (optional)**

1. Beat cream cheese and sugar in small bowl on medium speed of mixer until blended. Add egg, vanilla and almond extract; beat well. (Mixture will be thin.)

2. Stir in cherries and food color, if desired.

Marbled Cherry Brownies

White Chip Lemon Bars

1¼ cups all-purpose flour, divided
1 cup granulated sugar, divided
⅓ cup butter, softened
¾ cup HERSHEY'S Premier White Chips
2 eggs, slightly beaten
¼ cup lemon juice
2 teaspoons freshly grated lemon peel
Powdered sugar

1. Heat oven to 350°F. Stir together 1 cup flour and ¼ cup granulated sugar in medium bowl. Cut in butter with pastry blender until mixture resembles coarse crumbs. Press mixture onto bottom of 9-inch square baking pan.

2. Bake 15 minutes or until lightly browned. Remove from oven; sprinkle white chips over crust.

3. Stir together eggs, lemon juice, lemon peel, remaining ¼ cup flour and remaining ¾ cup sugar in medium bowl; carefully pour over chips and crust.

4. Bake 15 minutes or until set. Cool slightly in pan on wire rack; sift with powdered sugar. Cool completely. Cut into bars.   *Makes about 36 bars*

English Toffee Bars

2 cups all-purpose flour
1 cup packed light brown sugar
½ cup (1 stick) butter
1 cup pecan halves
Toffee Topping (recipe follows)
1 cup HERSHEY'S Milk Chocolate Chips

1. Heat oven to 350°F. Combine flour, brown sugar and butter in large bowl; mix until fine crumbs form. Press into ungreased 13×9-inch baking pan. Sprinkle pecans over crust. Drizzle Toffee Topping evenly over pecans and crust.

2. Bake 20 to 22 minutes or until topping is bubbly and golden. Remove from oven. Immediately sprinkle chocolate chips over top; press gently onto surface. Cool completely. Cut into bars.   *Makes about 36 bars*

Toffee Topping: Combine ⅔ cup butter and ⅓ cup packed light brown sugar in small saucepan. Cook over medium heat, stirring constantly, until mixture comes to boil; boil and stir 30 seconds. Use immediately.

White Chip Lemon Bars

Kickin' Brownies

½ cup hazelnuts or unblanched almonds
¾ cup butter
2 cups sugar
¾ cup cocoa powder
3 eggs, lightly beaten
2 teaspoons vanilla
1 cup all-purpose flour
1½ cups fresh or thawed frozen raspberries
    White Ganache (page 178)
    Chocolate Ganache (page 178)
3 to 4 tablespoons raspberry jam

1. Preheat oven to 350°F. To remove skins from nuts, spread in single layer on baking sheet. Bake 10 to 12 minutes or until skins begin to flake off; let cool slightly. Wrap hazelnuts in heavy kitchen towel; rub against towel to remove as much of skins as possible. Cool completely. Place hazelnuts in food processor. Process using on/off pulsing action until hazelnuts are finely chopped, but not pasty. Set aside.

2. Lightly grease 2 (8-inch) square baking pans. Line bottoms of pans with foil; lightly grease foil. Set aside.

3. Melt butter in medium saucepan over medium heat, stirring occasionally. Remove saucepan from heat. Stir in sugar and cocoa powder until well blended. Stir in eggs and vanilla until smooth. Stir in flour just until blended. Pour batter evenly into prepared pans. Press raspberries gently into batter.

4. Bake 15 to 20 minutes or until center is just set. Do not overbake. Cool brownies completely in pans on wire rack.

5. Run knife around edges of pans to loosen brownies. Gently work flexible metal spatula down edges and slightly under brownies to loosen from bottoms of pans. Hold wire rack over top of 1 pan; invert to release brownie. Remove foil; discard. Place cutting board or plate over brownie; invert brownie.

6. Prepare White Ganache and Chocolate Ganache. Reserve 2 tablespoons White Ganache; spread remaining White Ganache evenly over brownie. Spread raspberry jam on top of ganache.

7. Unmold remaining brownie as directed in Step 5. Place flat side down on bottom layer, pressing gently to seal. Spread Chocolate Ganache evenly over top layer. Drizzle reserved 2 tablespoons White Ganache over top. Sprinkle with hazelnuts. Cut into 16 squares. Store tightly covered in refrigerator up to 1 week. *Makes 16 brownies*

continued on page 178

Kickin' Brownies

White Ganache

**1 cup (6 ounces) white chocolate chips or chopped white chocolate,
   divided**
3 tablespoons whipping cream
½ teaspoon almond extract

1. Combine ½ cup white chocolate chips and whipping cream in medium saucepan. Heat over medium heat until chocolate is half melted, stirring occasionally.

2. Remove saucepan from heat. Stir in remaining ½ cup white chocolate chips and almond extract until mixture is smooth. Keep warm (ganache is semi-firm at room temperature).   *Makes ¾ cup ganache*

Chocolate Ganache

2 tablespoons whipping cream
1 tablespoon butter
**½ cup (2 ounces) semisweet chocolate chips or chopped semisweet
   chocolate**
½ teaspoon vanilla

1. Combine whipping cream and butter in small saucepan. Heat over medium heat until mixture boils, stirring frequently.

2. Remove saucepan from heat. Stir in chocolate chips and vanilla until mixture is smooth, returning to heat for 20- to 30-second intervals, as needed to melt chocolate. Keep warm (ganache is semi-firm at room temperature).
                                                    Makes ¾ cup ganache

Tri-Layer Chocolate Oatmeal Bars

Crust
- 1 cup uncooked rolled oats
- ½ cup all-purpose flour
- ½ cup firmly packed light brown sugar
- ¼ cup MOTT'S® Natural Apple Sauce
- 1 tablespoon margarine, melted
- ¼ teaspoon baking soda

Filling
- ⅔ cup all-purpose flour
- ½ teaspoon baking powder
- ¼ teaspoon salt
- ¾ cup granulated sugar
- ¼ cup MOTT'S® Natural Apple Sauce
- 1 whole egg
- 1 egg white
- 2 tablespoons unsweetened cocoa powder
- 1 tablespoon margarine, melted
- ½ teaspoon vanilla extract
- ¼ cup low fat buttermilk

Icing
- 1 cup powdered sugar
- 1 tablespoon unsweetened cocoa powder
- 1 tablespoon skim milk
- 1 teaspoon instant coffee powder

1. Preheat oven to 350°F. Spray 8-inch square baking pan with nonstick cooking spray. For crust, in bowl, mix oats, ½ cup flour, brown sugar, ¼ cup apple sauce, 1 tablespoon margarine and baking soda. Stir until coarse crumbs form. Press evenly into bottom of prepared pan. Bake 10 minutes.

2. For filling, in bowl, mix ⅔ cup flour, baking powder and salt. In large bowl, mix granulated sugar, ¼ cup apple sauce, whole egg, egg white, 2 tablespoons cocoa, 1 tablespoon margarine and vanilla. Add flour mixture alternately with buttermilk; stir until blended. Spread filling over baked crust. Bake 25 minutes or until toothpick inserted in center comes out clean. Cool completely.

3. To prepare icing, in bowl, mix powdered sugar, 1 tablespoon cocoa, milk and coffee powder until smooth. Spread over bars. Stand until set. Run tip of knife through icing to score. *Makes 14 servings*

Marshmallow Krispie Bars

1 (21-ounce) package DUNCAN HINES® Family-Style Chewy Fudge
    Brownie Mix
1 package (10½ ounces) miniature marshmallows
1½ cups semisweet chocolate chips
1 cup creamy peanut butter
1 tablespoon butter or margarine
1½ cups crisp rice cereal

1. Preheat oven to 350°F. Grease bottom only of 13×9-inch pan.

2. Prepare and bake brownies following package directions for cake-like recipe. Remove from oven. Sprinkle marshmallows on hot brownies. Return to oven. Bake for 3 minutes longer.

3. Place chocolate chips, peanut butter and butter in medium saucepan. Cook over low heat, stirring constantly, until chips are melted. Add rice cereal; mix well. Spread mixture over marshmallow layer. Refrigerate until chilled. Cut into bars. *Makes about 2 dozen bars*

Chewy Butterscotch Brownies

2½ cups all-purpose flour
1 teaspoon baking powder
½ teaspoon salt
1 cup (2 sticks) butter or margarine, softened
1¾ cups packed brown sugar
1 tablespoon vanilla extract
2 eggs
1⅔ cups (11-ounce package) NESTLÉ® TOLL HOUSE® Butterscotch
    Flavored Morsels, *divided*
1 cup chopped nuts

PREHEAT oven to 350°F.

COMBINE flour, baking powder and salt in medium bowl. Beat butter, sugar and vanilla extract in large mixer bowl until creamy. Beat in eggs. Gradually beat in flour mixture. Stir in *1 cup* morsels and nuts. Spread into ungreased 13×9-inch baking pan. Sprinkle with *remaining* morsels.

BAKE for 30 to 40 minutes or until wooden pick inserted in center comes out clean. Cool in pan on wire rack. Cut into bars.

Makes about 4 dozen brownies

*Marshmallow
Krispie Bars*

Baklava

4 cups slivered almonds and/or walnuts (1 pound)
1¼ cups sugar, divided
2 teaspoons ground cinnamon
¼ teaspoon ground cloves
1 package (16 ounces) frozen phyllo dough (about 20 sheets), thawed
1 cup butter, melted
1½ cups water
¾ cup honey
2 (2-inch-long) strips lemon peel
1 tablespoon fresh lemon juice
1 cinnamon stick
3 whole cloves

1. Place half the nuts in food processor. Process using on/off pulsing action until nuts are finely chopped, but not pasty. Remove from container. Repeat with remaining nuts. Combine nuts, ½ cup sugar, cinnamon and ground cloves in medium bowl; mix well.

2. Unroll phyllo dough and place on large sheet of waxed paper. Cut phyllo sheets in half crosswise to form 2 stacks, each about 13×9 inches. Cover phyllo with plastic wrap and clean, damp kitchen towel.

3. Preheat oven to 325°F. Brush 13×9-inch baking dish with some butter. Place 1 phyllo sheet in bottom of dish, folding in edges if too long; brush with butter. Repeat with 7 more phyllo sheets, brushing surface of each sheet with butter as they are layered. Sprinkle about ½ cup nut mixture evenly over layered phyllo.

4. Top nuts with 3 more layers of phyllo, brushing each sheet with butter. Sprinkle another ½ cup nut mixture on top. Repeat layering and brushing of 3 phyllo sheets with ½ cup nut mixture until there are a total of 8 (3-sheet) layers. Top final layer of nut mixture with remaining 8 phyllo sheets, brushing each sheet with butter.

5. Cut Baklava lengthwise into 4 equal sections, then cut diagonally at 1½-inch intervals to form diamond shapes. Sprinkle top lightly with water to prevent top phyllo layers from curling up during baking. Bake 50 to 60 minutes or until golden brown.

6. Combine water, remaining ¾ cup sugar, honey, lemon peel, lemon juice, cinnamon stick and whole cloves in medium saucepan. Bring to a boil over high heat. Reduce heat to low; simmer 15 minutes. Strain hot syrup; drizzle evenly over hot Baklava. Cool completely. *Makes about 32 pieces*

Almond Fudge Topped Shortbread

1 cup (2 sticks) butter or margarine, softened
½ cup powdered sugar
¼ teaspoon salt
1¼ cups all-purpose flour
2 cups (12-ounce package) HERSHEY'S Semi-Sweet Chocolate Chips
1 (14 ounce) can sweetened condensed milk (not evaporated milk)
½ teaspoon almond extract
½ cup sliced almonds, toasted

1. Heat oven to 350°F. Grease 13×9×2-inch baking pan.

2. Beat butter, powdered sugar and salt in large bowl until fluffy. Add flour; mix well. With floured hands, press evenly into prepared pan.

3. Bake 20 minutes or until lightly browned.

4. Melt chocolate chips and sweetened condensed milk in heavy saucepan over low heat, stirring constantly. Remove from heat; stir in extract. Spread evenly over baked shortbread. Garnish with almonds; press down firmly. Cool. Chill 3 hours or until firm. Cut into bars. Store covered at room temperature.

Makes 24 to 36 bars

Creamy Cappuccino Brownies

1 package (21 to 24 ounces) brownie mix
1 tablespoon coffee crystals *or* 1 teaspoon espresso powder
2 tablespoons warm water
1 cup (8 ounces) Wisconsin Mascarpone cheese
3 tablespoons sugar
1 egg
   Powdered sugar

Grease bottom of 13×9-inch baking pan. Prepare brownie mix according to package directions. Pour half of batter into prepared pan. Dissolve coffee crystals in water; add Mascarpone, sugar and egg. Blend until smooth. Drop by spoonfuls over brownie batter; top with remaining brownie batter. With knife, swirl cheese mixture through brownies creating marbled effect. Bake at 375°F 30 to 35 minutes or until toothpick inserted in center comes out clean. Sprinkle with powdered sugar.

Makes 2 dozen brownies

Favorite recipe from **Wisconsin Milk Marketing Board**

Candies &
Confections

Maple-Cashew Brittle

1 cup sugar
1 cup maple-flavored syrup*
¼ cup water
3 tablespoons butter
1½ cups lightly salted roasted cashews
¼ teaspoon baking soda

*Do not use pure maple syrup.

1. Lightly butter 15×10×1-inch jelly-roll pan.

2. Combine sugar, syrup, water and butter in heavy 2-quart saucepan. Bring to a boil over medium heat, stirring occasionally. Attach candy thermometer to side of pan, making sure bulb is submerged in sugar mixture but not touching bottom of pan. Continue boiling, without stirring, about 25 minutes or until mixture reaches hard-crack stage (300° to 305°F) on candy thermometer. (Watch carefully so that mixture does not burn.) Remove from heat; immediately stir in cashews and baking soda.

3. Immediately pour into prepared pan, quickly spreading to edges of pan and making sure cashews are spread in single layer. Cool completely, about 30 minutes. Break into pieces. Store in airtight container at room temperature up to 4 weeks. *Makes about 1¼ pounds brittle*

Traditional Nut Brittle: Substitute light corn syrup for maple-flavored syrup and deluxe mixed nuts without peanuts for cashews. Proceed as directed.

Maple-Cashew
Brittle

Triple Layer Fudge

Chocolate Fudge (recipe follows)
Peanut Butter Fudge (recipe follows)
White Fudge (recipe follows)

1. Grease 13×9-inch baking pan; set aside. Prepare Chocolate Fudge. Immediately spread in prepared pan with lightly greased rubber spatula.

2. Immediately prepare Peanut Butter Fudge; spread evenly over Chocolate Fudge with lightly greased rubber spatula.

3. Immediately prepare White Fudge; spread evenly over Peanut Butter Fudge with lightly greased spatula.

4. Cover fudge with plastic wrap. Refrigerate 2 hours or until firm. Cut into 1-inch squares. Store tightly covered in refrigerator up to 3 weeks.

Makes about 10 dozen pieces

Chocolate Fudge

1½ **cups granulated sugar**
  1 **can (5 ounces) evaporated milk**
  2 **tablespoons butter**
 ¼ **teaspoon salt**
1½ **cups miniature marshmallows**
  1 **cup (6 ounces) semisweet chocolate chips**
1½ **teaspoons vanilla**

1. Combine sugar, milk, butter and salt in medium saucepan. Bring to a boil over medium heat, stirring constantly. Boil 5 minutes, stirring constantly.

2. Remove saucepan from heat. Stir in marshmallows until melted and mixture is blended.

3. Add chocolate chips and vanilla. Stir until mixture is smooth. Stir mixture 6 minutes or until slightly thickened.

Peanut Butter Fudge: Reduce granulated sugar to ¾ cup; add ¾ cup packed light brown sugar. Prepare as directed for Chocolate Fudge in Steps 1 and 2, omitting butter. Substitute ½ cup creamy peanut butter for semisweet chocolate chips in Step 3 and proceed as directed.

White Fudge: Substitute white chocolate chips for semisweet chocolate chips. Prepare as directed for Chocolate Fudge.

Triple Layer Fudge

Candy Basket

Cookie Glaze (recipe follows)
2 tablespoons unsweetened cocoa powder
2 tablespoons powdered sugar
1 package (3.5 ounces) 3½-inch brown chocolate sticks
1 package (3.5 ounces) 3½-inch white chocolate sticks
1 round cardboard container (3-inch diameter)
Ribbon
Assorted small candies

1. Combine Cookie Glaze and cocoa in small bowl; mix until well blended. Stir in 2 tablespoons powdered sugar to thicken to proper spreading consistency.

2. Cover outside of cardboard container with foil; frost with thickened glaze. Place chocolate sticks, side by side, in frosting; let stand until hardened. Tie ribbon around "basket." Fill with assorted candies.   *Makes 1 basket*

Cookie Glaze: Combine 4 cups powdered sugar and 4 tablespoons milk in small bowl. Stir; add 1 to 2 tablespoons more milk as needed to make medium-thick, pourable glaze.

Toffee Diamonds

1 cup (2 sticks) I CAN'T BELIEVE IT'S NOT BUTTER!® Spread, softened
2 cups all-purpose flour
1 cup firmly packed brown sugar
1 egg, separated
½ teaspoon vanilla extract
1 cup chopped walnuts

Preheat oven to 325°F. Grease 15½×10½-inch jelly-roll pan; set aside.

In large bowl, with electric mixer, beat I Can't Believe It's Not Butter!® Spread, flour, sugar, egg yolk and vanilla until well blended. Evenly spread dough into prepared pan. With fork, beat egg white slightly. With pastry brush, brush egg white over top of flour mixture; sprinkle with walnuts.

Bake 30 minutes or until golden. Remove from oven and immediately cut into diamonds. Remove from pan to wire rack; cool completely.

Makes 4 dozen diamonds

Candy Basket

Toll House Famous Fudge

1½ **cups granulated sugar**
⅔ **cup (5 fluid-ounce can) NESTLÉ® CARNATION® Evaporated Milk**
 2 **tablespoons butter or margarine**
¼ **teaspoon salt**
 2 **cups miniature marshmallows**
1½ **cups (9 ounces) NESTLÉ® TOLL HOUSE® Semi-Sweet Chocolate**
    Morsels
½ **cup chopped pecans or walnuts (optional)**
 1 **teaspoon vanilla extract**

LINE 8-inch-square baking pan with foil.

COMBINE sugar, evaporated milk, butter and salt in medium, *heavy-duty* saucepan. Bring to a *full rolling boil* over medium heat, stirring constantly. Boil, stirring constantly, for 4 to 5 minutes. Remove from heat.

STIR in marshmallows, morsels, nuts and vanilla extract. Stir vigorously for 1 minute or until marshmallows are melted. Pour into prepared baking pan; refrigerate for 2 hours or until firm. Lift from pan; remove foil. Cut into pieces.

Makes 49 pieces

For Milk Chocolate Fudge: SUBSTITUTE 1¾ cups (11.5-ounce package) NESTLÉ® TOLL HOUSE® Milk Chocolate Morsels for Semi-Sweet Morsels.

For Butterscotch Fudge: SUBSTITUTE 1⅔ cups (11-ounce package) NESTLÉ® TOLL HOUSE® Butterscotch Flavored Morsels for Semi-Sweet Morsels.

For Peanutty Chocolate Fudge: SUBSTITUTE 1⅔ cups (11-ounce package) NESTLÉ® TOLL HOUSE® Peanut Butter & Milk Chocolate Morsels for Semi-Sweet Morsels and ½ cup chopped peanuts for pecans or walnuts.

Toll House Famous Fudge

Pecan Rolls

¼ **cup corn syrup**
¼ **cup water**
1¼ **cups sugar**
1 **egg white**
⅛ **teaspoon cream of tartar**
1 **teaspoon vanilla**
1 **package (14 ounces) caramels, unwrapped**
3 **tablespoons water**
2 **cups coarsely chopped pecans**

1. Line 9×5-inch loaf pan with buttered waxed paper; set aside. Combine corn syrup, water and sugar in heavy, small saucepan. Cook over medium heat, stirring constantly, until sugar dissolves and mixture comes to a boil. Wash down side of pan frequently with pastry brush dipped in hot water to remove sugar crystals. Carefully clip candy thermometer to side of pan (do not let bulb touch bottom of pan.) Continue to cook until mixture reaches the hard-ball stage (255°F).

2. Meanwhile, beat egg white and cream of tartar with heavy-duty electric mixer until stiff but not dry. Slowly pour hot syrup into egg white mixture, beating constantly. Add vanilla; beat until candy forms soft peaks and starts to lose its gloss. Spoon mixture into prepared pan. Cut into 3 strips lengthwise, then crosswise in center. Freeze until firm.

3. Line baking sheet with waxed paper; set aside. Melt caramels with water in heavy, small saucepan over low heat, stirring occasionally. Arrange pecans on waxed paper. Working quickly, drop 1 piece of frozen candy mixture into melted caramels to coat. Roll in pecans to coat completely and shape into log. Place on prepared baking sheet to set. Repeat with remaining candy pieces, reheating caramels if mixture becomes too thick.

4. Cut logs into ½-inch slices. Store in refrigerator in airtight container between layers of waxed paper or freeze up to 3 months.

Makes 6 (5-inch) rolls

Note: For perfect slices, freeze finished rolls before cutting.

Toasted Almond Truffles

½ cup NESTLÉ® CARNATION® Evaporated Milk
¼ cup granulated sugar
1¾ cups (11.5-ounce package) NESTLÉ® TOLL HOUSE® Milk Chocolate
   Morsels
½ to 1 teaspoon almond or vanilla extract
1 cup sliced almonds, finely chopped, toasted

COMBINE evaporated milk and sugar in small, *heavy-duty* saucepan. Bring to a *full rolling boil* over medium-low heat, stirring constantly. Boil, stirring constantly, for 3 minutes. Remove from heat.

STIR in morsels. Stir vigorously until mixture is smooth. Stir in almond extract. Refrigerate for 1½ to 2 hours. Shape into 1-inch balls; roll in nuts. Cover; refrigerate until ready to serve. *Makes about 2 dozen truffles*

Tiger Butter

1 pound white chocolate, broken into 1-inch pieces
1 jar (12 ounces) chunky peanut butter
6 ounces semisweet chocolate chips

Microwave Directions
Place white chocolate in 1½-quart microwavable bowl. Microwave on HIGH 3 minutes or until melted. Add peanut butter and microwave on HIGH 2 minutes or until mixture is smooth and creamy. Blend well. Spread mixture into 15½×10½-inch jelly-roll pan lined with waxed paper.

In 2-cup microwavable measuring cup, melt chocolate chips on HIGH about 2 minutes. Pour melted chocolate over peanut butter mixture; swirl with knife or drizzle melted chocolate over top of mixture using fine tip of pastry tube to make stripes. Chill until set. Cut into squares. *Makes 2 pounds candy*

Favorite recipe from **Texas Peanut Producers Board**

Mint Truffles

1 package (10 ounces) mint chocolate chips
⅓ cup whipping cream
¼ cup butter or margarine
1 container (3½ ounces) chocolate sprinkles

1. Line baking sheet with waxed paper; set aside. Melt chips with whipping cream and butter in heavy, medium saucepan over low heat, stirring occasionally. Pour into pie pan. Refrigerate until mixture is fudgy, but soft, about 2 hours.

2. Shape about 1 tablespoonful mixture into 1¼-inch ball. To shape, roll mixture between palms. Repeat procedure with remaining mixture. Place balls on waxed paper.

3. Place sprinkles in shallow bowl; roll balls in sprinkles. Place truffles in petit four or candy cups. (If sprinkles won't stick because truffle has set, roll truffle between palms until outside is soft.) Truffles may be refrigerated 2 to 3 days or frozen several weeks. *Makes about 24 truffles*

Tip: Truffles can also be coated with unsweetened cocoa, powdered sugar, chopped nuts, colored sprinkles or cookie crumbs to add flavor and prevent the truffle from melting in your fingers.

Peanut Butter Crunch Candy

1½ cups sugar
¾ cup dark corn syrup
1½ cups crunchy peanut butter
1 teaspoon vanilla
6 cups corn flakes
½ cup salted peanuts

Bring sugar and corn syrup to a rolling boil. Remove from heat and add peanut butter and vanilla. Stir to blend. Pour over corn flakes and peanuts and mix until all cereal is coated. Pat into 2 greased 8×8×2-inch pans. While still warm, cut into squares. *Makes 18 servings*

Favorite recipe from **Peanut Advisory Board**

Mint Truffles

Butter Almond Crunch

1½ cups HERSHEY'S Semi-Sweet Chocolate Chips or HERSHEY'S MINI
    CHIPS™ Semi-Sweet Chocolate Chips, divided
1¾ cups chopped almonds, divided
1½ cups (3 sticks) butter or margarine
1¾ cups sugar
  3 tablespoons light corn syrup
  3 tablespoons water

1. Heat oven to 350°F. Line 13×9×2-inch pan with foil; butter foil.

2. Sprinkle 1 cup chocolate chips into pan; set aside. Spread chopped almonds in shallow baking dish. Bake about 7 minutes or until golden brown, stirring occasionally; set aside.

3. Melt butter in heavy 3-quart saucepan; stir in sugar, corn syrup and water. Cook over medium heat, stirring constantly, to 300°F on a candy thermometer (hard-crack stage) or until mixture separates into hard, brittle threads when dropped into small amount of very cold water. (Bulb of candy thermometer should not rest on bottom of saucepan.)

4. Remove from heat; stir in 1½ cups toasted almonds. Immediately spread mixture evenly over chocolate chips in prepared pan; do not disturb chips. Sprinkle with remaining ¼ cup toasted almonds and remaining ½ cup chocolate chips; cool slightly.

5. Score candy into 1½-inch squares with sharp knife, wiping knife blade after drawing through candy. Cool completely; remove from pan. Remove foil; break candy into pieces. Store in airtight container in cool, dry place.

Makes about 2 pounds candy

gift tip

These are just the right treats to say "Thank you," or "Great job!" Place individual candy pieces in paper or foil candy cups. Candy cups are available in a variety of colors at stores which carry cake decorating supplies.

Butter Almond Crunch

Layered Mint Chocolate Fudge

Prep Time: 20 minutes • **Chill Time:** 2 hours 20 minutes

1 (12-ounce) package semi-sweet chocolate chips
1 (14-ounce) can EAGLE® BRAND Sweetened Condensed Milk (NOT
    evaporated milk), divided
2 teaspoons vanilla extract
1 cup (6 ounces) premium white chocolate chips *or* 6 ounces white
    confectionery coating*
1 tablespoon peppermint extract
   Few drops green or red food coloring, if desired

White confectionery coating can be purchased in candy specialty stores.

1. Line 8- or 9-inch square pan with waxed paper. In heavy saucepan over low heat, melt semi-sweet chocolate chips with 1 cup Eagle Brand. Stir in vanilla. Spread half the mixture in prepared pan; chill 10 minutes or until firm. Keep remaining chocolate mixture at room temperature.

2. In heavy saucepan over low heat, melt white chocolate chips with remaining Eagle Brand. Stir in peppermint extract and food coloring, if desired. Spread over chilled chocolate layer; chill 10 minutes or until firm. Spread reserved chocolate mixture over mint layer. Chill 2 hours or until firm.

3. Turn fudge onto cutting board; peel off paper and cut into squares. Store loosely covered at room temperature.   *Makes about 1¾ pounds fudge*

Chocolate Peanut Butter Fudge

 ½ cup butter or margarine, melted
1½ cups SMUCKER'S® Creamy Natural Peanut Butter
 3 cups powdered sugar
 ½ cup firmly packed brown sugar
1½ teaspoons vanilla
 1 cup (6 ounces) semi-sweet chocolate chips
 ⅓ cup butter or margarine

Combine ½ cup butter, peanut butter, powdered sugar, brown sugar and vanilla; mix well. Press mixture into 13×9-inch pan.

Melt chocolate chips and ⅓ cup butter. Spread over peanut butter mixture. Refrigerate until firm. Cut into 1-inch squares.   *Makes 60 bars*

Layered Mint
Chocolate Fudge

Peppermint Taffy

2 tablespoons butter, softened and divided
½ cup powdered sugar
2½ cups granulated sugar
½ cup water
¼ cup distilled white vinegar
7 to 8 drops red food coloring
½ teaspoon peppermint extract

1. Butter 12-inch ceramic oval platter or dish with 1 tablespoon butter. Line large baking sheet with foil; sprinkle evenly with powdered sugar.

2. Combine granulated sugar, water, vinegar and remaining 1 tablespoon butter in heavy 2- or 2½-quart saucepan. Bring to a boil, stirring frequently. Attach candy thermometer to side of pan, making sure bulb is submerged in sugar mixture but not touching bottom of pan. Continue boiling, without stirring, about 10 minutes or until sugar mixture reaches between hard-ball stage (265°F) and soft-crack stage (270°F) on candy thermometer. Remove from heat; stir in food coloring and peppermint extract.

3. Slowly pour hot sugar mixture onto prepared platter. Let stand 20 to 25 minutes or until cool enough to handle and an indent made with your finger holds its shape.

4. Remove all jewelry as candy will stick to it. With liberally buttered hands, carefully pick up taffy and shape into a ball. (Center of candy may still be very warm but will cool quickly upon handling.) Scrape up any taffy that sticks to plate with rubber spatula.

5. Begin to pull taffy between your hands into thick rope about 18 inches long while turning and twisting taffy back on itself. Continue pulling taffy about 10 to 15 minutes or until it lightens in color, has satiny finish and is stiff. (It is important to be patient and pull taffy long enough or it will be sticky.)

6. When taffy begins to hold the folds of the rope shape and develops ridges in the rope, begin pulling 1-inch-wide ropes from taffy and let ropes fall onto prepared powdered sugar surface. Cut each rope with buttered kitchen shears. Cut taffy ropes into 1-inch pieces using shears. Cool completely; wrap pieces individually in waxed paper. Store in airtight container at room temperature up to 1 week.   *Makes about 1 pound taffy*

Lemon Taffy: Substitute 4 to 5 drops yellow food coloring for red food coloring and lemon extract for peppermint extract. Proceed as directed.

Peppermint and Lemon Taffy

Nut Brittle

½ cup peanut butter, toasted cashew butter or toasted almond butter
1 teaspoon baking soda
1 teaspoon vanilla
1 cup sugar
1 cup light corn syrup
2 tablespoons water
1½ cups raw peanuts, cashews or unblanched almonds
½ cup butter or margarine

1. Melt peanut butter in top of double boiler over medium heat, stirring constantly. Reduce heat to low. Let stand, stirring occasionally.

2. Lightly grease 16×14-inch or very large baking sheet. Set aside. Blend baking soda and vanilla in small bowl until smooth.

3. Combine sugar, corn syrup and water in saucepan. Bring to a boil over medium-high heat, stirring constantly. Add nuts and butter. Return to a boil, stirring constantly. Reduce heat to medium. Boil until temperature registers 280°F on candy thermometer, stirring constantly.

4. Remove saucepan from heat. Stir in peanut butter until well blended. Stir in vanilla mixture until well blended. Immediately pour mixture evenly over prepared baking sheet.

5. Quickly roll out brittle with buttered rolling pin to as thin as possible. Cool completely on baking sheet. Break into pieces. Store tightly covered at room temperature for up to 1 week.   *Makes about 1½ pounds brittle*

gift tip

Create a gift basket that will make nut lovers go wild! Simply package this delicious brittle with Cashew & Pretzel Toffee Clusters (page 10), Spicy Toasted Nuts (page 34), and Chocolate Macadamia Nut Chippers (page 116).

Nut Brittle

German Chocolate No-Cook Fudge

3 packages (4 ounces each) German sweet chocolate, broken into pieces
1 cup (6 ounces) semisweet chocolate chips
1 can (14 ounces) sweetened condensed milk
1 cup chopped pecans
2 teaspoons vanilla
36 pecan halves (optional)

1. Butter 8-inch square pan; set aside. Melt chocolate and chips in heavy, small saucepan over very low heat, stirring constantly. Remove from heat. Stir in condensed milk, chopped pecans and vanilla until combined. Spread in prepared pan. Arrange pecan halves on fudge. Score fudge into squares with knife. Refrigerate until firm.

2. Cut into squares. Store in refrigerator. Bring to room temperature before serving.

Makes about 2 pounds fudge

Easy Rocky Road

2 cups (12-ounce package) HERSHEY'S Semi-Sweet Chocolate Chips
¼ cup (½ stick) butter or margarine
2 tablespoons shortening (do *not* use butter, margarine, spread or oil)
3 cups miniature marshmallows
½ cup coarsely chopped nuts

1. Butter 8-inch square pan.

2. Place chocolate chips, butter and shortening in large microwave-safe bowl. Microwave at HIGH (100%) 1 to 1½ minutes or just until chocolate chips are melted and mixture is smooth when stirred. Add marshmallows and nuts; blend well.

3. Spread evenly in prepared pan. Cover; refrigerate until firm. Cut into 2-inch squares. Cover; store in refrigerator.

Makes 16 squares

German Chocolate No-Cook Fudge

Classic English Toffee

 1 cup unsalted butter
 1 cup sugar
 2 tablespoons water
 ¼ teaspoon salt
 1 teaspoon vanilla
 1 bar (3 ounces) premium semisweet chocolate, broken into small pieces
 1 bar (3 ounces) premium bittersweet chocolate, broken into small pieces
 ½ cup chopped toasted pecans

1. Line 9-inch square pan with heavy-duty foil, leaving 1-inch overhang on sides.

2. Combine butter, sugar, water and salt in heavy 2- or 2½-quart saucepan. Bring to a boil over medium heat, stirring frequently. Attach candy thermometer to side of pan. Continue boiling about 20 minutes or until sugar mixture reaches hard-crack stage (305° to 310°F) on candy thermometer, stirring frequently. (Watch closely after temperature reaches 290°F, because temperature will rise quickly and mixture will burn above 310°F.) Remove from heat; stir in vanilla. Immediately pour into prepared pan, spreading to edges. Cool completely.

3. Microwave chocolates in small microwave-safe bowl on MEDIUM (50% power) 5 to 6 minutes or until melted, stirring every 2 minutes.

4. Remove toffee from pan to flat surface. Lay foil flat; spread chocolate evenly over toffee. Sprinkle chocolate with pecans, pressing lightly with fingertips so pecans adhere to chocolate. Refrigerate about 35 minutes or until chocolate is set. Bring to room temperature before breaking toffee.

5. Carefully break toffee into pieces without dislodging pecans. Store in airtight container at room temperature between sheets of waxed paper.

Makes about 1¼ pounds toffee

Classic English Toffee

Foolproof Dark Chocolate Fudge

Prep Time: *10 minutes* • ***Chill Time:*** *2 hours*

3 cups (18 ounces) semi-sweet chocolate chips
1 (14-ounce) can EAGLE® BRAND Sweetened Condensed Milk (NOT
    evaporated milk)
    Dash salt
½ to 1 cup chopped nuts, if desired
1½ teaspoons vanilla extract

1. Line 8- or 9-inch square pan with foil. Butter foil; set aside.

2. In heavy saucepan over low heat, melt chips with Eagle Brand and salt. Remove from heat; stir in nuts, if desired, and vanilla. Spread evenly in prepared pan.

3. Chill 2 hours or until firm. Turn fudge onto cutting board; peel off foil and cut into squares. Store covered in refrigerator.

Makes about 2 pounds fudge

Marshmallow Fudge: Substitute 2 cups miniature marshmallows for nuts. Stir in 2 tablespoons butter with vanilla. Proceed as directed above.

Festive Black or White Peanut Clusters

1 cup (6 ounces) semisweet chocolate chips or white chocolate
½ cup creamy peanut butter
1 teaspoon shortening
1 cup roasted peanuts

Microwave Directions
Place chocolate in 1½-quart microwavable dish. Microwave on HIGH 2 to 3 minutes or until melted. Add peanut butter and shortening; microwave on HIGH 1 to 2 minutes or until mixture is smooth and creamy. Blend well. Stir in peanuts. Drop by teaspoonfuls onto waxed paper-lined cookie sheet; chill until set. Store in refrigerator.

Makes 2 dozen clusters

Favorite recipe from **Texas Peanut Producers Board**

Foolproof Dark Chocolate Fudge

Hazelnut Cream Bonbons

3 cups hazelnuts (about 1 pound)
½ cup butter, divided
¼ cup whipping cream
1 teaspoon vanilla
1 package (1 pound) powdered sugar, sifted

1. Preheat oven to 350°F. To remove skins from hazelnuts, spread in single layer on baking sheet. Bake 10 to 12 minutes until toasted and skins begin to flake off; cool slightly. Wrap hazelnuts in heavy kitchen towel; rub against towel to remove as much of the skins as possible. Cool completely. Reserve 1½ cups hazelnuts.

2. Place remaining 1½ cups hazelnuts in food processor; add 2 tablespoons butter. Process using on/off pulsing action until hazelnuts are coarsely ground. Set aside.

3. Beat remaining 6 tablespoons butter and cream in large bowl with electric mixer at medium speed until smooth. Beat in vanilla and ground hazelnut mixture. Add sugar, 1 cup at a time, beating until well combined. Turn mixture out onto countertop. Knead until mixture forms a ball. Roll out mixture to ¼-inch thickness with rolling pin. Cut into small heart shapes with cookie cutter. Reroll dough scraps and cut out more hearts.

4. Place remaining hazelnuts in food processor; process using on/off pulsing action until finely chopped. Spread hazelnuts on waxed paper. Coat hearts with hazelnuts, pressing to adhere. Store in airtight container at room temperature between sheets of waxed paper.   *Makes about 8 dozen bonbons (2 pounds)*

Chocolate-Dipped Hazelnut Cream Bonbons: Prepare bonbons as directed using only 1½ cups hazelnuts and omitting hazelnut garnish in step 4. Melt 18 ounces (3 cups) semisweet chocolate chips in top of double boiler over hot, not boiling, water. Dip hearts halfway in chocolate; place on waxed paper. Let stand until chocolate is set. Store as directed.

Hazelnut Cream Bonbons

Butterscotch Patties

1 cup packed light brown sugar
¼ cup butter
2 tablespoons dark corn syrup
1 tablespoon water
1 tablespoon cider vinegar
Pinch salt

1. Line 2 baking sheets with foil.

2. Combine all ingredients in heavy 2-quart saucepan. Bring to a boil over medium-high heat, stirring constantly.

3. To wash down sugar crystals, dip pastry brush in hot water. Gently brush crystals down into sugar mixture or let them collect on brush bristles. Dip brush frequently in hot water to clean off bristles.

4. Continue boiling about 15 minutes or until sugar mixture reaches hard-crack stage (300° to 305°F) on candy thermometer, stirring frequently. (Watch carefully so that mixture does not burn.) Remove from heat; stir until mixture stops bubbling.

5. Quickly drop teaspoonfuls onto prepared baking sheets to form patties. Cool patties completely, about 15 minutes. Store in airtight container at room temperature between sheets of waxed paper.

Makes about 3 dozen (1½-inch) patties (about ½ pound)

Butterscotch Pieces: Prepare sugar mixture as directed. Pour onto foil instead of dropping into patties; cool completely and break into pieces. Store as directed.

gift tip

Present this old-fashioned candy in a pretty tin or a decorated paper or fabric hatbox. Before filling the container with the candy, line it with colorful tissue paper.

Butterscotch Pieces

After-Dinner Mocha Truffle Cups

36 Chocolate Cups (page 216) or purchased chocolate liqueur cups
1 cup whipping cream
2 eggs*
1 package (6 ounces) semisweet chocolate chips
2 tablespoons prepared espresso, cooled
1 tablespoon coffee-flavored liqueur
1 teaspoon unflavored gelatin
  Sweetened whipped cream
  Chocolate-covered coffee beans and fresh mint leaves for garnish

*Use only grade A clean, uncracked eggs.

1. Prepare Chocolate Cups; set aside.

2. Place large bowl and beaters from electric mixer in freezer until cold. Pour whipping cream into chilled bowl. Beat with electric mixer at high speed until soft peaks form. Refrigerate.

3. Place eggs in separate large bowl; beat with electric mixer at high speed about 5 minutes or until thick and lemon colored.

4. Melt chocolate chips in top of double boiler over hot, not boiling, water. Uncover; stir until chocolate is melted. Remove from heat. Add ¼ cup melted chocolate to beaten eggs; stir to blend. Stir egg mixture into remaining melted chocolate. Cook over medium heat 1 minute, stirring constantly. Remove from heat.

5. Place espresso and liqueur in small saucepan; sprinkle with gelatin. Let stand 1 minute to soften. Gradually add gelatin mixture, a few drops at a time, to chocolate mixture, whisking until smooth.

6. Gently fold ½ of chocolate mixture into chilled whipped cream. Add to remaining chocolate, gently folding until combined. Spoon chocolate mixture into Chocolate Cups with small spoon, filling to top; refrigerate at least 3 hours or until firm.

7. To serve, dollop with sweetened whipped cream. Garnish, if desired.

Makes 36 candy cups (about 1½ pounds)

continued on page 216

After-Dinner Mocha Truffle Cups

Chocolate Cups

1 package (12 ounces) semisweet chocolate chips
1 tablespoon vegetable shortening
   Small, clean craft paintbrush

1. Melt chips with shortening in heavy small saucepan over low heat, stirring constantly to prevent scorching. Remove from heat as soon as chocolate melts.

2. Spoon about ½ tablespoon melted chocolate into each of 36 small foil candy cups. Brush chocolate up side of each cup with small, clean craft paintbrush, coating foil completely. Carefully wipe off any chocolate that may have run over top of foil cup using tip of finger. Place cups on baking sheet; let stand in cool place until firm. (Do not refrigerate.)

3. To remove foil cups, cut slits in bottom of foil cups and peel foil up from bottom. (Do not peel down from top edge.)   *Makes 36 cups*

Milk Chocolate Almond Brickle

1¼ cups almonds, toasted and coarsely chopped
   1 cup (2 sticks) butter
1½ cups packed brown sugar
1¾ cups (11.5-ounce package) NESTLÉ® TOLL HOUSE® Milk Chocolate Morsels

SPRINKLE nuts over bottom of well-greased 13×9-inch baking pan.

MELT butter in medium, *heavy-duty* saucepan over medium heat. Stir in sugar. Bring to a boil, stirring constantly. Boil, stirring constantly, for 7 minutes. Pour hot mixture over nuts; let stand for 5 minutes. Sprinkle with morsels. Let stand for 5 minutes or until morsels are shiny and soft; spread evenly.

REFRIGERATE for about 20 minutes. Break into bite-size pieces.
                                        Makes about 50 pieces

Chocolate-Covered
Almond Apricot Tussies

Prep Time: *40 minutes* • ***Cook Time:*** *1½ minutes* • ***Chill Time:*** *1 hour*

  2 cups vanilla wafer crumbs (about 60 wafers, crushed)
  1 cup finely chopped almonds
  ⅓ cup HERSHEY₂S Cocoa
  1 can (14 ounces) sweetened condensed milk (not evaporated milk)
  1 package (8 ounces) dried apricots, chopped
  ½ cup chopped candied cherries
  ¼ teaspoon almond extract
  2 cups (11.5-ounce package) HERSHEY₂S Milk Chocolate Chips
  4 teaspoons shortening (do *not* use butter, margarine, spread or oil)

1. Line small muffin cups (1¾ inches in diameter) with paper bake cups.

2. Combine crumbs, almonds and cocoa in large bowl. Add sweetened condensed milk, apricots, cherries and almond extract; mix well. Refrigerate 30 minutes. Roll mixture into 1-inch balls; press into prepared muffin cups.

3. Place chocolate chips and shortening in medium microwave-safe bowl. Microwave at HIGH (100%) 1½ minutes; stir. If necessary, microwave at HIGH an additional 15 seconds at a time, stirring after each heating, just until chips are melted when stirred. Spoon about 1 teaspoon melted chocolate over each filled cup. Refrigerate until chocolate is set. Store, covered, in refrigerator.

Makes about 6 dozen candies

Tip: When melting chocolate, even a small amount of moisture may cause it to "seize" or become stiff and grainy. Chocolate can sometimes be returned to melting consistency by adding 1 teaspoon solid shortening (do not use butter, margarine, spread or oil) for every 2 ounces of chocolate and reheating it.

Acknowledgments

The publisher would like to thank the companies and organizations listed below for the use of their recipes and photographs in this publication.

Arm & Hammer Division, Church & Dwight Co., Inc.

California Dried Plum Board

Canada's Canola Industry

Cherry Marketing Institute

ConAgra Foods®

Dole Food Company, Inc.

Duncan Hines® and Moist Deluxe® are registered trademarks of Aurora Foods Inc.

Eagle® Brand

Filippo Berio® Olive Oil

Fleischmann's® Yeast

Grandma's® is a registered trademark of Mott's, Inc.

Heinz North America

Hershey Foods Corporation

The Hidden Valley® Food Products Company

Lawry's® Foods

© Mars, Incorporated 2003

McIlhenny Company (TABASCO® brand Pepper Sauce)

Mott's® is a registered trademark of Mott's, Inc.

National Honey Board

Nestlé USA

Newman's Own, Inc.®

Peanut Advisory Board

Pear Bureau Northwest

Reckitt Benckiser Inc.

The J.M. Smucker Company

The Sugar Association, Inc.

Property of © 2003 Sunkist Growers, Inc. All rights reserved.

Texas Peanut Producers Board

Unilever Bestfoods North America

Walnut Marketing Board

Washington Apple Commission

Wisconsin Milk Marketing Board

Index

METRIC CONVERSION CHART

VOLUME MEASUREMENTS (dry)

1/8 teaspoon = 0.5 mL
1/4 teaspoon = 1 mL
1/2 teaspoon = 2 mL
3/4 teaspoon = 4 mL
1 teaspoon = 5 mL
1 tablespoon = 15 mL
2 tablespoons = 30 mL
1/4 cup = 60 mL
1/3 cup = 75 mL
1/2 cup = 125 mL
2/3 cup = 150 mL
3/4 cup = 175 mL
1 cup = 250 mL
2 cups = 1 pint = 500 mL
3 cups = 750 mL
4 cups = 1 quart = 1 L

VOLUME MEASUREMENTS (fluid)

1 fluid ounce (2 tablespoons) = 30 mL
4 fluid ounces (1/2 cup) = 125 mL
8 fluid ounces (1 cup) = 250 mL
12 fluid ounces (1 1/2 cups) = 375 mL
16 fluid ounces (2 cups) = 500 mL

WEIGHTS (mass)

1/2 ounce = 15 g
1 ounce = 30 g
3 ounces = 90 g
4 ounces = 120 g
8 ounces = 225 g
10 ounces = 285 g
12 ounces = 360 g
16 ounces = 1 pound = 450 g

DIMENSIONS

1/16 inch = 2 mm
1/8 inch = 3 mm
1/4 inch = 6 mm
1/2 inch = 1.5 cm
3/4 inch = 2 cm
1 inch = 2.5 cm

OVEN TEMPERATURES

250°F = 120°C
275°F = 140°C
300°F = 150°C
325°F = 160°C
350°F = 180°C
375°F = 190°C
400°F = 200°C
425°F = 220°C
450°F = 230°C

BAKING PAN SIZES

Utensil	Size in Inches/Quarts	Metric Volume	Size in Centimeters
Baking or Cake Pan (square or rectangular)	8×8×2	2 L	20×20×5
	9×9×2	2.5 L	23×23×5
	12×8×2	3 L	30×20×5
	13×9×2	3.5 L	33×23×5
Loaf Pan	8×4×3	1.5 L	20×10×7
	9×5×3	2 L	23×13×7
Round Layer Cake Pan	8×1½	1.2 L	20×4
	9×1½	1.5 L	23×4
Pie Plate	8×1¼	750 mL	20×3
	9×1¼	1 L	23×3
Baking Dish or Casserole	1 quart	1 L	—
	1½ quart	1.5 L	—
	2 quart	2 L	—